{ Finding Common Ground }

For Library of
Kennedy School of
Government from
Dave Bishop

D1496495

FINDING COMMON GROUND

The Art of Legislating
in an Age of Gridlock

DAVE BISHOP

Foreword by Lori Sturdevant
Afterword by John Hughes

MINNESOTA
HISTORICAL
SOCIETY PRESS

www.mnhspress.org

The Minnesota Historical Society Press is a member of the Association of American University Presses.

Manufactured in the United States of America

10 9 8 7 6 5 4 3 2 1

♾ The paper used in this publication meets the minimum requirements of the American National Standard for Information Sciences—Permanence for Printed Library Materials, ANSI Z39.48–1984.

International Standard Book Number
ISBN: 978–0–87351–979–3 (paper)
ISBN: 978–0–87351–980–9 (e-book)

Library of Congress Cataloging-in-Publication Data

Bishop, Dave, 1929– author.
Finding common ground : the art of legislating in an age of gridlock / Dave Bishop ; foreword by Lori Sturdevant ; afterword by John Hughes.
   pages   cm
   Includes bibliographical references and index.
   ISBN 978-0-87351-979-3 (pbk. : alk. paper) — ISBN 978-0-87351-980-9 (ebook)
   1. Bishop, Dave, 1929– 2. Minnesota—Politics and government—1951–
3. Legislators—Minnesota—Biography. 4. Minnesota. Legislature—
Biography. I. Title.
   F610.3.B57A3   2015
   328.73'092—dc23
   [B]   2015028418

This and other Minnesota Historical Society Press books are available from popular e-book vendors.

Contents

Foreword *by Lori Sturdevant*   vii

Preface   xv

CHAPTER 1: The Scourge of Partisanship   3
   CASE: Constituent Protection

CHAPTER 2: Building Bridges   17
   CASE: Winning with the Lottery
   CASE: The Importance of Trust

CHAPTER 3: Power Sharing   33
   CASE: Sexual-Predator Politics
   CASE: Community-Notification Struggle

CHAPTER 4: The Power of the Conference Committee   57
   CASE: A Bonding Maneuver

CHAPTER 5: Legislating and the News Media   69
   CASE: Northwest Airlines and a Sales Tax

CHAPTER 6: Lawmakers Get an Idea, Now What?   79
   CASE: The Living Will

CHAPTER 7: The Tricky Dance   99
   CASE: Moving the Historical Society

CHAPTER 8: The Legislator's Toolbox   109
    CASE: Changing the Speed Limit
    CASE: The Minority Amendment That Moved
        a Majority's Mountain
    CASE: Legislative Failures

Conclusion   131

Afterword *by John Hughes*   135

Acknowledgments   145

Notes   147

Index   153

Picture Credits   160

{ Foreword }

Lori Sturdevant

I was out of the country in December 2002 when Minnesotans learned the breathtaking depth of the fiscal hole into which their state government had tumbled. The post–9/11 recession had combined with oversized tax cuts in 1999–2001 to produce a massive forecasted deficit in the next biennial state budget. "It's $4.5 billion!" my news-attuned eleven-year-old daughter reported when I called home. "And some Republican legislator is calling on the new governor to raise taxes."

I didn't have to ask for names. The new governor was Republican Tim Pawlenty, elected that fall on a vow of "no new taxes." And the surest suspect among Republican legislators to call on Pawlenty to break that vow in the face of unprecedented budget trouble was Representative Dave Bishop of Rochester—the fellow you'll meet on the pages that follow.

Unfortunately for Minnesota, Bishop was a lame duck that December. He'd chosen not to run for an eleventh term in 2002. But he had not fallen silent. Upon my return, I found Bishop as unreserved as ever in sharing his prescriptions for Minnesota's betterment. When I wrote a column suggesting that the state's dire new circumstances warranted a change in Pawlenty's position, Bishop willingly contributed his own argument for a tax increase.

"I've been there," said the outgoing chair of the house Ways and Means Committee. "I've tried to turn off every spending faucet there is. I don't believe you can restrict the outflow enough to balance the budget with spending cuts alone." He also confessed his regret about recommending a cut in the state's reserve funds the session before, when he thought recurring surpluses during what today is remembered as the "dot-com bubble" would endure indefinitely. Bishop recommended a cigarette tax increase that eventually became law, and a sales tax on clothing that has not—yet.

I called Bishop "endearingly outspoken" in that 2002 column for the *Minneapolis Star Tribune.* This book is proof that thirteen years later, he still is. He has little use for reticence when the public's interest is the matter at hand. But he was never a politician to grab a microphone, seek a headline, or write a book for his own sake.

Bishop was a rare sort among legislators. His focus was lawmaking, not partisan politics. He is exceptionally able, and was often in the thick of efforts to solve major problems. He is an independent thinker who did not shrink from attention-getting controversy. Yet he is uncommonly disinterested in self-promotion. Through ten house terms he took care to avoid eclipsing others. Bishop's selflessness was an asset to his effectiveness, enhancing his ability to gain the trust of his colleagues.

It's also an ingredient in this book. The lawmaking handbook that follows is a fruit of Bishop's generosity. It is a gift and guide to serious American lawmakers who want to be effective despite partisan gridlock or minority status. The lessons he conveys are well tested, and often were acquired through the school of hard knocks. They aren't shortcuts. Bishop didn't believe in them. But they are affirmations that even in the highly partisan environment that was (and is) the Minnesota House, attention to the basics brings rewards. What basics? Homework enough to acquire deep familiarity with the issues at hand and the rules of lawmaking. Commitment to meeting constituents' needs. Respect for all comers to the capitol. Friendships that reach across the aisle. And a sincere desire to make the state one serves a better place.

Bishop's love for Minnesota runs deep. That may be in part because he is what I call "an adult convert to Minnesota," one who arrived as a young adult and caught the spirit of state-building that has enlivened Minnesota since the middle of the nineteenth century. Bishop came for the reason many do—he was in love with a Minnesotan who wanted to return home. Born in Syracuse, New York, in 1929, Bishop was pursuing a law degree at Cornell University in Ithaca when he became smitten with fellow student Bea Habberstad of Rochester, Minnesota. They married the year he graduated, 1954; he has made her hometown his own ever since.

Bishop's young adult years were occupied establishing a successful general law practice, investing in Rochester real estate, raising five children with Bea, and dabbling in Republican politics, an interest since his Hamilton College days as an English composition and political science major. He was so successful financially that he was able to retire from full-time practice of law in 1976 and step up his civic and political activities.

He and I first met in connection with the latter. It was 1980, the year the Reagan Revolution swept Republican politics. Bishop was one of Minnesota's thirty-four delegates to the national GOP convention in Detroit in mid-July; I was the *Minneapolis Tribune* reporter assigned to cover the delegation. Tall, gregarious, and no great fan of nominee Ronald Reagan, Bishop was a standout in the group even before he joined forces with like-minded delegates from Hawaii, Michigan, and Massachusetts to try to force a roll-call vote on the party platform on Tuesday night. They wanted a chance to register their opposition to a platform that had taken a sharp turn to the right on social issues, opposing both legal abortion and the Equal Rights Amendment for women.

Bishop was making headway among Minnesota delegates with a petition calling for a roll-call vote when Minnesota's Reagan co-chair, Marsie Leier of Roseville, caught wind of his insurgency. He was within four votes of the number of signatures he needed when Leier persuaded several who had signed it to remove their names. She convinced the delegation's co-chair, Governor Al Quie—a former congressman from the district that includes Rochester, and Bishop's friend—to refuse to sign. Bishop was beaten. He was angry enough to make himself scarce at the convention for a few hours. He thought about leaving for home, he confessed to me the next day. He hated being reduced to a bit player in a television show—a role national convention delegates in both parties have been consigned to play ever since that year.

Bishop's anger flared but subsided quickly—a pattern that legislative observers would see repeated in future years. He decided he could not leave the convention and miss being a witness to history. On Thursday he enjoyed cheering for Reagan's vice presidential choice, George H. W. Bush—likely in part because Reagan's selection of the more moderate Bush was a disappointment to the Minnesota delegation's more conservative wing.

The memory of that episode made me pleased to see Bishop arrive in the Minnesota House in January 1983 as the new representative from Rochester. I knew that he was affable, approachable, and a "good quote." He had shown that he was a political centrist, unafraid to buck the prevailing conservative winds in his party. He was clever enough to use procedural tools from which others might shrink, or of which others were ignorant, to strive to make a difference. And, at age fifty-four that year, he was at a station in life that allowed him to make legislative service nearly a full-time occupation, despite the position's purported part-time status and modest pay. I knew he would be one to watch.

That hunch was soon confirmed, as the stories in the chapters that follow reveal. By the end of his twenty-year legislative career, he had been chief author of more than two hundred bills and amendments that had been signed into law. That's prodigious productivity for any legislator, let alone one who served in the minority caucus for fourteen of those twenty years. It's more noteworthy still when one knows the wide range and controversial nature of the topics Bishop tackled, from sex offender community notification to environmental protection to living wills to Native American treaty rights.

Some readers may approach Bishop's story thinking that he describes a bygone era in American politics, one in which bipartisan collaboration was more easily accomplished. The stories that follow ought to disabuse them of that notion. It's true that the philosophical divide between Republicans and DFLers (the Democratic-Farmer-Labor Party) today is wider than ever. But even before the Minnesota legislature's caucuses took party designation in 1974, bipartisan lawmaking was not easy. Working with legislators in the opposite caucus was always viewed with suspicion; openly breaking with one's caucus on a major issue was always uncommon. It risked the loss of prestige, influence, and/or party endorsement.

Bishop endured at least a taste of all of that bitter medicine at one time or another. His legislative achievements required the courage of his convictions, which he had in abundance. More to the point: they also required the support of attentive, engaged constituents who had Bishop's back, regardless of his standing with legislative leaders or his party.

That's where every reader of this book can see himself or herself in Bishop's story. His Rochester constituents should know that their votes made his service possible. Their continuing support through the varied political winds of two decades allowed him to persevere even when he was in the doghouse with his party's conservative base. Only twice, in his first election and his last one, did Bishop win with less than 58 percent of the vote in District 30B; in most elections he captured two of every three votes. A loyal base can do much to inspire legislative courage.

I suspect many readers of this book will put it down saying, "I wish we had more Dave Bishops in the legislature today." That sentiment should be more than an idle wish. It should be a spur to action. Dave's story should inspire readers to get involved in politics, recruit people of his caliber to run for office, and back them with time, treasure, and votes.

Lori Sturdevant, *Minneapolis Star Tribune* columnist, has written and edited several books of Minnesota history, including *Her Honor: Rosalie Wahl and the Minnesota Women's Movement.*

Representative Dave Bishop at the Minnesota State Capitol, about 1987

{ Preface }

People sometimes seem allergic to state politics. In certain ways, that is easy to understand. Writing, arguing, and passing legislation is a complicated process, full of disappointments and compromises, carried out by hardworking people with big egos and even bigger goals. I know this because I was one of them. But the process is, quite simply, tied to *who we are* as Americans.

We are taught in grammar school that American government is a democracy. If you break apart the word, you'll find the Greek roots *demos*, or people, and *cracy*, meaning rule, power, or government. President Abraham Lincoln, without ever actually using the word "democracy" in his Gettysburg Address, defined it best as "government of the people, by the people, for the people." America's founders had feared centralized power. They wanted to separate and distribute authority in their new government. So the Constitution established a bicameral or two-chambered legislature, including the house and the senate, to create the nation's laws. This basic structure required legislative collaboration because both chambers take a pass at drafting a new law, and the wording of the two attempts must eventually agree. But it's not all about collaboration across the aisle: members of political parties also organize themselves into caucuses, where they select candidates for leadership positions, come to agreement on policies, and then act together to wield greater influence.

As our nation has come of age, something has gone astray in our governmental process. State and federal governments are suffering from gridlock. This logjam has been caused by the excessive partisanship of individual ideologues and doctrinaire pressure groups that spend billions of dollars to influence elections. While the country has endured other eras of hyperpartisanship, the centralization and size of these power groups have created a new political climate in which lawmakers who use negotiation and bipartisan compromise to enact laws for the common good are punished in reelections. The 2010 US Supreme Court decision on the Citizens United case allowed corporations and unions to be treated legally as persons in regard to campaign contributions, thus abolishing the previous funding limits. The result is that politically motivated organizations are interfering with the goals of and constitutional structure intended by our nation's founders. The "government of the people, by the people, for the people" described by Lincoln is increasingly becoming a fiction.[1]

Simply put, we are losing our democracy. Legislatures, state and federal, are so deadlocked in partisanship that little serious legislating is getting done. Lawmakers make speeches to put each other down rather than try to work together. They prioritize showing each other up while failing to produce real changes that benefit the public. Instead of yielding to constitutional pressures to collaborate across branches of government and political parties, they restrict themselves to the negative approach of carping and criticizing. This is particularly true among members of the minority party. This method is sterile, focusing only on the next election and doing nothing to look for common ground as a base for new legislation. Simply voting "no" on every proposal, opposing every action the majority takes, shirks a legislator's obligation to represent the entire population of their district or state. The public expects all its legislators to work together for the good of the whole community.

This inability of legislators to solve problems has led to citizen apathy and disillusionment, and a negative public view of the legislative process. I am deeply disturbed by this. I see little respect for the important process of genuine deliberation and group decision-making on matters of common public interest.

There is a better way. The solution is group work, the formation of alliances across chasms of political identifications and competing interests. Crossing these chasms can be hazardous and tricky. Bridges spanning the divides are fragile. But successful group work can be done. Members of the minority caucus can gain the support of the majority for an idea and see it through successfully.

This book shows how. It describes how legislators, particularly those in the minority party, can find common ground and be effective without having the formal majority power often needed to create change. The book outlines techniques I used to get support from those who had the power to help or kill my bills. Descriptions of these techniques are followed by case examples showing how the approaches worked to enact legislation. There are also examples of failures so that policymakers can see firsthand the pitfalls to avoid.

The stories and conversations come from my memory, of course, and others may remember events differently; I have checked the facts as best I can.

Finding Common Ground is the product of my twenty years of experience in the Minnesota legislature, only six of which I spent as a member of the majority. During my time in the minority, I successfully guided more than two hundred bills and amendments into law. I approached my work in what I believed to be the correct way for getting things done, a method other legislators can learn. I will show how practical and natural this approach is, and how essential it is to democracy.[2]

My goals are: (1) to show minority and majority lawmakers ways to achieve bipartisan success; (2) to strengthen our democracy by increasing public understanding and support for a positive legislative process; and (3) to increase public respect for the complex work of legislators and legislatures.

My target audience is policymakers from all walks of life, in all partisan or nonpartisan governing bodies that make decisions by majority. These include school and township boards, city councils, county boards, and state and federal legislatures. I also hope to provide a better understanding of the process of lawmaking for political scientists and others who are interested in effective, nonpartisan, bipartisan, and ethical legislating, be they high-school civics teachers, college instructors in political science, elected legislators, or the general public.

A legislator's top priority should be any legislative need of his or her district's constituents. The next priority is caucus priority and partisan bills. The third priority is the legislator's own ideas, worked into nonpartisan bills that will need support from both sides. With success in passing these generally good bills, the legislator gains regard from his colleagues, which will help him when he needs assistance with his own district's bills.

Political professionals understand the tradeoffs involved in cooperation, negotiation, and compromise. The goal is to represent the interests of all constituents. But if necessary, a legislator will choose to prioritize the needs of constituents in his or her own district over the needs of people from other districts. Legislators realize that other members have distinct goals, like these, that reflect honest partisan beliefs; a proposal or a compromise may include a member's hidden agendas. Legislators do not expect each other to be transparent, and they are not surprised by unfriendly amendments that are intended to embarrass or other partisan ploys. They understand that those in the leadership of both parties can and will bury bills that they don't like or don't understand. These challenges are all part of doing the work. But legislators also have to stick to their word. And because legislators are human beings working together, we find it easier to see the viewpoints of those who have previously helped us out of a jam. In fact, my success in developing political influence allowed me to respond more effectively to the needs of my own constituents.

Passing legislation is and should be difficult, and it takes the work of both parties, in all their complexities, to do it right. I offer the thoughts in this book in hopes of assisting in that process.

{ Finding Common Ground }

CHAPTER I

{ # The Scourge of Partisanship }

I'm a pragmatist. As a lawyer in general practice for more than twenty years, my strength was in facilitating compromise and settling cases. Whether I was handling a divorce, a neighborhood dispute, or an accident, I always tried to see both sides.

I remember taking a case to a court trial. When the judge asked if the parties had exhausted all avenues for settlement, I asked for a recess. I went into a conference room with the other attorney, a well-respected man named Art Swan.

I said, "Let's trade files."

He was pretty surprised. My suggestion was just an idea that had popped into my head. It was a novel approach, possible only because I knew there was nothing confidential in my file. But by reading each other's files we would learn just how strong the other was, and the transparency of the exchange built trust. Settlement therefore became a satisfactory compromise.

I handled many divorce cases—over a hundred, I'm sure. When no other lawyer was involved, I met with the two parties, either together or separately, to hear their stories. I listened to both sides, looking for common ground on which to mediate a solution. I had seen that by getting divorced, people often traded one misery for another. My goal in many cases was to negotiate a compromise that would allow the marriage to be restored. I loaned the couples books to read that offered suggestions for overcoming marital conflict. Unfortunately, many legislators don't have the predisposition to seek compromise. They seem to wholeheartedly support, or completely oppose, any particular idea. More and more, their commitment to ideology overrules their commitment to solving legislative problems. As legislators they can't be persuaded to listen and absorb, change their thinking, or alter their vote for a collaborative compromise. For these partisans, there is no middle ground. These are the conditions where gridlock becomes inevitable.

Many of these ideologues belong to the minority party, where they play an opposition role, seemingly content to attack the majority without ever accomplishing anything themselves. They don't try to approach the majority to build relationships and bridges. This is especially true as reelection time approaches and the political environment becomes intensely partisan.

After I won my first election in 1982, I was excited to join the Minnesota House of Representatives as a Republican in the minority. I traveled to the capitol in St. Paul, eager to get busy and start legislating. I wanted to make a difference, and I immersed myself in the job. I read everything I could and sought advice from veteran legislators. I tried to gain knowledge about the process and learn fast how to get things done.

One day, I visited a senior legislator in my caucus. I noticed he had nothing on his desk, no papers anywhere. "How do you do this?" I asked. "I'm just swamped by everything that comes into my office." "I'm a member of the minority," the legislator said. "It's not my responsibility to carry things forward, unless I happen to be the chief author on a bill. I look things over when they come in, then I throw them out. That's how I keep my desk clear."

I realized that the empty desktop meant this legislator wasn't involved. He was a critic, and a capable one at that, but while he was in the minority he never took responsibility for anything.

I also realized that if I adopted this legislator's approach as a minority member, I'd be ineffective and bored stiff. I had come to the legislature to pass laws. I had ideas for change.

Not long after my conversation with that legislator, I was in the house retiring room preparing an amendment for printing and distribution on the floor. That's when a senior representative of my caucus approached me.

"What are you doing?" he asked.

"I have an amendment for this bill," I said.

"Why?" he asked. "Vote against it. Just vote it down. Don't help it."

"The bill needs to be fixed," I said. "I have an idea that will fix it, that will help it get passed into law."

"We should not be helping the majority," my colleague replied. "We want to prevent the majority from doing good bills so that we have a chance to take over ourselves."

"No," I said. "If I see the purpose of the bill is good, then

I have to try to fix it, because otherwise the majority might pass it, and we'll end up with defective legislation."

My friend was unpersuaded. "Unless voters see bad legislation passed by the majority, they won't be willing to shift power to the minority," he said. "We have to let the majority make mistakes, so we can point to the errors and justify defeating them in the next election."

Despite what he told me, I went ahead and offered the amendment. I was never good at taking suggestions from senior lawmakers when I thought they were wrong, though I was happy to work with them. Looking back, I don't remember what the amendment, or the underlying bill, was about— but I do remember that both were approved.

I was struck by the conversation. It showed the difference between a legislator who wanted to make and pass laws and one who didn't want to help the majority. This is the conflict that exists for all legislators. Do you support your caucus while in the minority and refuse to help the majority in such a way that would make the other party look good? Or do you collaborate with the majority on nonpartisan bills that benefit the whole state? These are two entirely separate political styles. A policymaker has to choose whether to be a positive force for enacting legislation or to form a wall of opposition with his or her caucus.

I know the path I preferred the great majority of the time.

And I wasn't alone. In 1991, the term of the University of Minnesota regent from my congressional district was due to expire. A minimum of two candidates were to be nominated for any such position by the Regent Candidate Advisory

Council. The council, created in 1988, was an attempt to take political favoritism out of the regent selection. It improved the method of selection by seeking qualified nominees, conducting extensive interviews, and making recommendations to the legislature. A long-standing tradition then allowed the district's legislators to meet and endorse a candidate from among the council's nominees.[1]

Since the majority of legislators from our district were Republicans, the advantage would have been given to our choice, Dr. Bryan Neel. But the joint house-senate Education and Finance Committee, controlled by the Democratic-Farmer-Labor (DFL) majority, supported another candidate, and tried to slam-dunk the process. The meeting for just the legislators from our district had been canceled, leaving the endorsement decision up to the joint committee.

I went to Bob Vanasek, then house speaker, and asked him to step in.

Vanasek and I had already developed a mutual respect which had started when he brought an amendment to me and asked me to offer it to a conference committee I was on. I did and it succeeded. Now I had a problem and I needed him to help. I argued that the procedure of shifting committees to gain partisan approval was unfair. I needed Vanasek to delay the legislative election for two weeks to give Dr. Neel time to lobby the full house and senate.

Vanasek then went to the senate majority leader, Roger Moe, and the two agreed to my request.

This was the type of bipartisan leadership Vanasek showed. He gave the minority the same respect as he did the majority. By empowering the minority, the majority leadership created an environment which encouraged discourse and included the people who would otherwise be disenfranchised. True democracy requires that lawmaking bodies integrate minority and majority party members to overcome partisanship. Creating or changing laws is hard work and requires input from many sources. It should end with bipartisan legislating that overcomes gridlock.

The minority should not see its only role as to embarrass the majority. It is important that majority and minority members form friendly relationships and help each other on matters that do not compromise caucus-identified positions. Minority members should offer positive bills for policy problems and support reasonable majority offerings that are nonpartisan. When a majority member's basic idea is sound and needs a slight adjustment, the minority member should participate as a coauthor or offer an amendment as a solution.

Most legislative proposals are not partisan. They are based on needs expressed by groups within a community or state. Many of the proposals are corrective in nature. They create licensing, start a program, or increase funding or fees. They might deal with new crimes, increase penalties, or create a park. Some could name a building, improve a highway, or clean up a river.

It is important to note, of course, that working across party lines to resolve policy issues does not absolutely preclude minority-caucus members from also engaging in legitimate blocking efforts. Minority-caucus members should feel free to offer troubling amendments—partisan amendments intended to embarrass the other party in the next election—

to majority bills, be they on welfare reform, the budget, or taxes, on occasion. Minority members know the amendments will not pass, and may not even want them to pass. Instead, the proposals are aimed at getting good press and becoming stones in the shoes of majority members. These partisan activities are legitimate political actions. Partisanship is part of the role of the minority, which must try to make itself look more politically attractive to the public at the next election.

However, as I've said, posturing for the next election is not the only role of the minority. Minority members who want to pass bills and create good public policy can be very effective if they are willing to downplay their partisanship. They need to try negotiation with partisan or moderate majority members. Such negotiations can lead to an agreement to work together as coauthors of good nonpartisan bills.

As a legislator, when I got involved in an issue, I always wanted to understand what the other side was looking for in a negotiation. What were the main points that needed to be included in the proposal in order for the deal to be a "win" for them? Compromise only gets a bad name when the parties have not been able to prove their results to be a win for each side. I looked for ways to negotiate where everyone felt like they left with what they needed.

In the current political climate, negotiations that could lead to compromise seem to be politically dangerous, and crossing the partisan chasm—even using independent judgment—can lead to punishment. In politics, as in physics, every action will provoke a reaction.

I have seen excessive partisanship cause defeats within

the partisans' own party, especially when the candidate is a moderate. In 1962, I was a volunteer vote counter representing Governor Elmer Andersen in his reelection contest against Karl Rolvaag. I counted thousands of paper ballots in Preston for Fillmore County and saw at least two hundred ballots that voted straight Republican but left a blank vote for governor. The election was the most closely divided in Minnesota history. Andersen lost to Rolvaag by ninety-one votes—out of more than 1.2 million cast.[2]

I was surprised to see so many citizens voting against their own party's governor. When I realized that these few absent Republican votes had caused Andersen to lose his reelection, I searched for a reason why the voters had strayed. What I found was that Andersen had appointed Democratic lawyer Robert Sheran to the supreme court. This bipartisan act, I concluded, had angered enough Republicans to cost him the reelection.

A similar thing happened in Rochester in the 1982 First District Republican endorsing convention. The delegates refused to endorse Congressman Arlen Erdahl because Erdahl did not have a perfect record of support for Republican President Ronald Reagan's legislative agenda. This led to the election of Tim Penny, the first-ever Democrat to represent our district. Clearly, narrow-minded partisanship had had a counterproductive political effect.

CASE: Constituent Protection

The legislative majority will usually permit passage of a minority member's bills for constituent services. However, this changed in 1983, my first session. In July 1978, my hometown of Rochester, built on the Zumbro River, had suffered a devastating flood. A once-in-more-than-a-century storm had dumped six inches of rain in six hours. Flash flooding on the Zumbro sent water into homes and blocked or destroyed roads and bridges. Five people died, and $60 million of damage was done. Citizens were shocked. It took years for the city to recover.[3]

The Chamber of Commerce and people from all over the city formed a task force to prevent damage from such a terrible flood in the future. In 1982, the task force recommended that the city ask the legislature for authority to levy a half-percent sales tax to pay for bonds funding the city's share of a huge flood-control project. Another half-percent levy would pay for improvements to Rochester's civic center.[4]

Minnesota had enacted a prohibition against local sales taxes in 1971. Under this prohibition only the state legislature could authorize a new local sales tax, usually to fund a specific project. The special law must contain a deadline, which is usually the time necessary for the tax to generate enough revenue to pay the general obligation bonds.[5]

In the 1982 general election, the voters of Rochester were asked to vote whether to ask the state permission to levy these two sales taxes. They both won, with 67 percent approval for the civic center and 72 percent for the city's share of flood control. In my mind, I had a mandate. Clearly, it was the responsibility of the newly elected legislators from Rochester, Gil Gutknecht and myself, to get the sales taxes approved.

I went to the state capitol ready to do what was necessary to get Rochester the taxes it wanted, but I quickly found out

Sixth Avenue and Fourth Street Southeast in Rochester, looking west, after a devastating flood hit the city on July 5, 1978. The damage demonstrated the need for a flood control system.

that legislators in both caucuses were not in a collaborative mood. The Democratic majority had announced a plan to pass major increases in sales and income taxes, and house Republicans had taken a caucus position against it.

As soon as I was settled into the State Office Building, next to the capitol, I got an appointment to see house speaker Harry Sieben, who was against including the "piggy-back" taxes. I told him I would need the support of the majority caucus for my constituents to get the sales taxes.

Sieben told me, "Your caucus has taken a position against our tax bill. I'll see that the authorization for the Rochester sales taxes gets put into the tax bill, but I'll need two Republican votes for the bill in order for that to happen." Sieben's offer was legitimate, and allowed me to respond to urgent constituent needs.

"I'll see what I can do," I said. Now I had a clear commitment which would put Rochester's new sales taxes into law.

I went to Gil Gutknecht. He and I faced a tough decision to either vote against our caucus position or reject our city's election mandate. However, in politics, you don't often get what's ideal or perfect. This was the only way the majority would give us the taxes. Hopefully it would prove a tolerable exception to the caucus position.

"This is the deal," I told Gutknecht. "For two Republican votes in favor of the tax bill we can get Rochester's one percent of sales-tax increases."

"Okay," Gutknecht quickly said. "Make the deal."

I went back to Sieben and told him we had an agreement. He could count on two votes from the Republican caucus.

Forty-five minutes later, Gutknecht came to my office.

"Dave," he told me, "you have to break the deal. I've really been bothered by the idea that I would go against the caucus and vote for a bill with big increases in income and sales taxes. I've thought about it, and I can't do it."

Ideologically, it was too hard for Gutknecht. I knew Rochester leaders would be upset if he refused to carry out our mandate, but Gutknecht held to his stance. He was always consistent in his conservative positions.

"Gil," I said, "I don't have to break the deal. I didn't promise your vote. I promised two Republican votes. What you've done is make me go find another vote."

"Well, all right," Gutknecht said, and he left.

I spoke with quite a few Republicans but had no luck. Finally, about 10 p.m. the next day, I wound up in the bar at the Kelly Inn near the capitol complex where several legislators from rural parts of the state stayed during sessions. I found Doug Carlson, a Republican from Sandstone who had political guts, and told him about my situation.

"Don't worry, Dave," Carlson said. "I'll be your second vote." Later, Don Frerichs, who had been twice elected from the Rochester Township area, came to see me and said, "Dave, you don't have to use Doug Carlson to vote for the tax bill. He's at risk in a heavily Democratic district. I'll do it."

Frerichs was prepared to risk his reputation in order to shield other Republicans from losing political face over the bill. This vote would later cause him to lose a primary vote for reelection.

With my two Republican votes locked up, the Rochester taxes were inserted into the bill by a house-senate conference committee. During the committee meeting, Sieben rescinded his opposition to the Rochester sales taxes, explaining that Frerichs and I had been helpful on other fiscal matters. The omnibus tax bill was approved 70–61 in the house and 40–26 in the senate and was signed into law by Governor Rudy Perpich.[6]

With the Rochester sales taxes approved by the state, the federal delegation from Minnesota went into action. The newly elected congressman representing Rochester, Tim Penny, and the rest of Minnesota's federal delegation succeeded in persuading congressional colleagues to make Rochester flood control a priority. The US Army Corps of

Engineers would ultimately put $97 million into Rochester flood control. More than $16 million in local sales taxes were collected through 1992 to pay for the city's share.[7]

As this flood-control plan was put into effect, about two thousand homes and businesses in Rochester were removed from the floodplain. A network of trails and parks was created along with seven flood-control reservoirs, all of which boosted recreational opportunities. By 1995, the project was complete.

In August 2007, another huge summer storm dumped six to twelve inches over a twenty-four-hour period into the Zumbro River watershed. Such a rain supposedly occurs only once every five hundred years. This storm caused enormous damage in Zumbro Falls, downstream from Rochester. In Rochester itself, however, no lives were lost. Buildings, streets, and parks survived intact.

The two-vote deal that led to a $100-million flood-control project had kept Rochester dry.

CHAPTER 2

{ Building Bridges }

I 've always believed there are three, not two, caucuses in any lawmaking body: the majority, the minority, and the members of both sides who build bridges. The bridge-building caucus is essential to successful government because of the way our public bodies have been established.

The US Constitution, as well as the constitution of Minnesota, wisely structures the legislative branch with two separate bodies, a house and a senate. Each of those bodies includes a majority and a minority caucus. This means that the legislative branch, itself just one part of the three-legged stool of government, has two majorities and two minorities.

This structure makes it hard, however, to pass laws and budgets. It creates genuine conflicts that must be resolved by negotiation and compromise in an effort to serve the best interests of the nation or the state. We must have lawmakers on both the local and federal levels who can go beyond election claims, political-party platforms, and the demands of party officers. They need to be problem solvers with the skills to resolve inevitable conflicts so the business of government can move forward.

Compromising requires mutual listening and deliberation. Reaching a compromise means balancing complex competing interests. Negotiators will need to understand both sides well in order to explain the merits of each and persuade the legislators necessary for support of the compromise. This process is essential to good government because democracy requires representation of multiple opinions.

Passing legislation is group work. It's a collegial practice. Success for legislators depends on networking, finding the persons who will have the greatest impact on whether a proposal is adopted. Networking enables legislators to create relationships they can use for information and power sharing. These relationships often cross party lines. Minority lawmakers in particular can't stick with only their own side or territory and expect to succeed. For minority members to find common ground, they must build bridges to the majority.

All of a legislator's colleagues are potential members of a team that a legislator can call upon to pursue his or her agenda. These people have various strengths, and those who have demonstrated their intelligence and dedication are particularly valuable. By reaching out, legislators will discover colleagues with different experiences, surprising perspectives, and common principles. This group should take every opportunity to discuss values and goals, and they may discover many commonalities.

As guidelines for the building of bridges or formation of coalitions to cross these partisan chasms, the minority members may ask themselves some basic questions: Whom do I look to for support? Whom do I look to for authority? Whom do I look to for leadership? There is a distinct difference between leadership and authority. What will they need to know from me, from others? When do I bring in the media?

When do I bring in the other body? What could go wrong, and how would I fix it?

The most successful alliances are based on respect and friendship, not political debts. Relationships are the keys to building bridges. A personal relationship has to exist for even a temporary bridge to be built. What makes the connection last is trust and confidence gained through collaboration.

Lawmakers will need to keep alert for opportunities to be helpful with others' agendas. This means looking over bills as they are published, listening to presentations, and being inquisitive about others' interests.

Another good way to be helpful is to privately point out potential weaknesses in others' proposals. Legislation is not different from other human interactions. People remember when someone has helped them with discretion and tact and they often feel a willingness to reciprocate, even when there is no duty or agreement to do so.

Contrary to popular belief, legislators rarely trade votes. They don't say, "I'll vote for your bill if you'll vote for mine." Communication is more sophisticated than that. Legislators help each other because they want to. Any suspicion that helping fellow members is part of some deal or contract brings disfavor and disdain to the process. For the most part, legislators try to avoid coming under such suspicion.

Legislating must involve a high level of civility. Legislators should be considerate of each other, even when they are directly opposed. Minority legislators should seek out members of the majority in natural situations and make as many friends as possible. They will probably find people with interests similar to theirs. Whether it is going to lunch, having a beer together, or taking a committee tour while crammed into a state van, time spent socializing is valuable groundwork for developing working relationships. I often left my house office complex to go over to the capitol cafeteria and seek out senators. I would sit down to eat with them, bend their ears, and listen to what they were working on. Until legislators do these things, they will never know their opposition well enough to build bridges.

Another way for legislators to get to know each other is through pleasant social events, where they can meet and talk to each others as individuals. Many good pieces of legislation have resulted from events that brought together two people who otherwise would not have met or had an opportunity to get to know each other.

Legislators can offer each other the valuable benefit of their ideas and judgment, which are brought pointedly into focus by their legislative agenda and efforts. With an open and friendly personality, legislators can use their ideas to persuade. The successful bridge builder is the legislator who brings both of these elements together: someone who is respected by both sides and liked as well.

CASE: Winning with the Lottery

In 1987, I was in the retiring room behind the Minnesota House of Representatives chamber. Representatives can step off the house floor into this room and have a discussion, grab a cup of coffee, or use the phone. On this particular day, I saw two of my colleagues having an intense conversation.

As I walked toward them, I heard Representative Willard

Munger, the dean of the house delegation, say, "Those bastards!" He was speaking with a fellow longtime DFL representative, Wayne Simoneau. "I'm really disgusted!" Munger continued.

As a minority Republican, I wasn't privy to the inner workings among senior Democrats, but since I liked both men that didn't stop me from entering the conversation. "What bastards, Willard?" I asked.

"My colleagues!" Munger said angrily. "The Democrats on the Rules Committee won't let my bill get to the floor. It's passed all the committees, but they won't let me get it through Rules."

No bill gets to the floor for a final vote until it gets approved by the Rules Committee, which was tightly controlled by the majority. Many controversial bills went to Rules to die.

I asked Munger why Rules Democrats didn't like his bill.

"They don't like the lottery, and they don't want all the money to go to an environmental trust fund," he said.

The lottery *was* controversial. Minnesota was no different from many other states in the 1980s. It was looking for new revenue sources for the state budget. Many legislators hated the idea of a lottery because they viewed it as a form of gambling, which encouraged addiction. They also thought the lottery took advantage of people.

I viewed the games as a good revenue source. "The lottery doesn't bother me, Willard," I told him. "Maybe I can help you."

"You're in the minority, Bishop," Munger replied. "How can you help me? You're not even on the Rules Committee."

"I don't know, Willard, but you have a good bill. There ought to be a way to get it out. I have some majority friends on Rules. Why don't you let me talk to some of them?"

"Okay," Munger said. "It won't do any harm, so go ahead."

I took a couple of days and contacted some Rules members I knew. "What's the problem with Munger's bill?" I asked.

Some voiced a concern about gambling. "I just don't like the lottery," one said.

Another said, "What is with this Environment and Natural Resources Trust Fund? Willard wants all the money from the lottery tied up in this fund, and I don't like that."

Munger's grand idea was to sequester lottery revenues into a trust fund that would be used only for environmental projects in the state. He was passionate about environment conservation and had distinguished himself in the legislature on the issue.

As I thought about ways to pry Munger's bill out of Rules, I realized there wasn't much I could do about the members' discomfort with the idea of the lottery as gambling. However, I did see a way to win votes on the revenue part of the proposal, although at a steep price for Munger. My plan was to cut the funds into three parts. Munger would have to give up two-thirds of what he wanted and designate its use for other purposes.

First, one-third of the lottery funds would go to the Greater Minnesota Corporation. The legislature had established this public corporation to develop new industries in the state, particularly in rural areas. It was a pet project of the governor, Rudy Perpich. We had tapped into the state reserve for most of the $106 million the legislature had ini-

Minnesota lottery game tickets, 1999

tially dedicated for the corporation. I figured that if we used a third of lottery proceeds to fund this endeavor going forward, it would satisfy those who worried that the GMC would be a continuing drain on state reserves.[1]

Another third of lottery proceeds would be funneled into

the state's reserve. This would satisfy Republicans who worried about potential tax increases. We didn't have any source of reserve money for the state at that time. This was a great weakness that had hit us hard in the early 1980s, when the state had pretty much run out of money.

That left the final third for Munger's Environmental and Natural Resources Trust Fund.[2]

I went back to him and said, "Willard, would you take less of the money for your trust fund if we can get the lottery bill passed?" I told him about my idea. He said he was willing to give it a try.

Next I returned to the Rules Committee members I had spoken with earlier. One was Rick Krueger, a Democrat from Staples. His desk had been next to mine on the house floor during my first year, and we had become good friends. I outlined the three-way split of lottery proceeds, and Krueger said he would support it.

I then talked to Representative Ann Wynia, the speaker pro tem. She said, "I don't like a lottery, but I guess if we're going to have one, this is a pretty good use for it." She said she would vote for it.

I spoke with a few more Rules Committee members who said they would support the plan. Then I went back to Munger. "Willard, I've got enough votes. Let's do an amendment."

"Okay," he said, "you do it."

I drafted the amendment and gave it to Munger to present to Rules. "No, Bishop," he told me—he never called me Dave in all the years I knew him. "You did the work. You offer it."

At the Rules hearing, Munger put a chair next to him, for me as we sat before the panel.

"Members of the committee," Munger began, "Representative Bishop is going to present the amendment to my bill for me."

In my twenty years in the legislature, this was the only time I recall appearing before the Rules Committee on such a controversial bill. "This is how it will get divided up," I told the panel, describing the distribution. "We're hoping you will support it."

They did. The house voted 69–63 to propose a constitutional amendment authorizing a state lottery. Then the lottery action shifted to the senate, where the companion bill passed 37–28. I served on the conference committee that worked out the differences between the house and senate versions. The conference committee changed funding allocation from thirds to fifty-fifty, increasing the Environmental and Natural Resources Trust Fund and Greater Minnesota Corporation shares at the expense of any share for the reserve.[3]

The original plan for a three-way split had ended the Rules Committee logjam and got the bill out of Rules to the floor and to the conference committee.

In 1988, a few months after the legislature concluded its work on the lottery bill, I was at my lake home in Wisconsin. The phone rang. It was Munger. He said Governor Perpich was planning a ceremonial lottery-bill signing at a park in Munger's hometown of Duluth.

"Bishop," Munger said, "I want you there."

"Okay, Willard, I'll come," I said.

Munger never forgot that I had stepped up and helped him. From then on, he asked me to sign onto all of his bills. The conversation I began with Munger in the retiring room resulted in a strong bridge between a powerful Democrat and a minority Republican, a bridge which made it possible for me to implement many important ideas.

The lottery games have been a fixture in Minnesota ever since. By 2015, the lottery had raised over $2.4 billion for the environment and the needs of the state's people.

CASE: The Importance of Trust

Trust is the most important foundation for building bridges. It is established by being straightforward and honest. Confidence in a colleague's judgment and opinions, and in the accuracy of their information, is the second-most important building block.

The number-one enemy of the legislator is distrust. Deceit, wrong information, or poor communication will sink a legislator quickly. The impact can be lasting. Personal credibility is a legislator's main currency. It doesn't take long for legislators to realize that a colleague knows what he or she is doing and can be trusted—or vice versa.

Just as trust brings success, distrust brings failure.

This truth struck home on two particular occasions where I was threatened or actually defeated in legislative efforts. In the first, I was approached by attorney Barbara Bloomer, a bar association specialist. She showed me an example of a durable power of attorney for financial matters. Her idea was that the same concept could apply to health care, legally authorizing a third party to make medical decisions when a grantor was no longer competent. I decided to offer the idea as an amendment germane to a bill that was then moving through committees in the house.

I went to the chief author, Representative Mike Jaros from Duluth, and said, "Mike, this amendment would fit with your bill and it is a good idea. People need a durable power." He said, "Fine, put it on."

I offered it as an amendment on the floor, which is very unusual, and Jaros accepted it. Normally a bill should go through the committee process so legislators and lobbyists can understand the proposal and have an opportunity for input. But I had already achieved a significant success in sponsoring the living will legislation, which I will discuss in a later chapter, and my reputation was such that Jaros agreed to let me circumvent the process. He took my word for it that the amendment would be good law.

I had used an Iowa law as a pattern, changing just a few things, and thought the piece of legislation was very simple. The Jaros bill passed the house with my amendment.

However, my failure to use the usual process created a problem. When the house bill went to conference, Bloomer and my lead supporters from the living will, the senior-citizen lobbyists, showed up to oppose it. I was shocked and felt blindsided. Because I had not kept them up to date with the process, my former supporters didn't trust me. The bill didn't have their fingerprints on it and they had not passed it through their own membership. As a result, my senate chief author, DFL senator Ember Reichgott Junge, said to me during the conference hearing, "I'm not comfortable with this; it hasn't gone through the proper people."

Reichgott Junge was also very worried about Minnesota Citizens Concerned for Life (MCCL). The group was the most feared political force in the 1985 state legislature. A veteran legislator once told me that MCCL was so powerful it could count on about 100 of the 134 house representatives to align with them on their positions. This was because they were so well organized and diligent in lobbying legislators and in candidate selection.

But MCCL didn't appear to be in opposition to this bill. I had already told the group, "This is fine. Don't worry about it. I'm not going to try to put any special provisions in here that you would be surprised by."

The MCCL lobbyist, Jackie Schwietz, had said, "All right, as long as we can trust you not to play games with it, we won't oppose it."

Like Reichgott Junge, the senior-citizen organizations expected MCCL to oppose the amendment—so when MCCL didn't, the seniors became suspicious that I had made an accommodation of some sort with one of their major opponents. This resulted in their further lack of support for the bill in conference.

I said to Representative Howard Orenstein, my chief supporter, "Let's take the amendment off. I don't want to have Mike Jaros lose his bill. We've lost and the senate has won."

Trust had collapsed. When a bicameral legislature is at work, trust is what is needed to get your bill to the governor. In this situation, the failure occurred because of the process, not because of the proposal. By trying to shortcut the process, I had created suspicion among my necessary supporters, both in the legislature and in the public. In fact, I learned that the process itself is an important part of building the trust required to pass legislation.

I pulled the amendment off the Jaros bill and offered it as a new, separate bill the next session. It went through normal procedures and passed in the house and senate.

A similar issue of trust was at play in another case, the second occasion I mention above. In 1993 the state Department of Natural Resources asked the legislature to approve a legal settlement with the Mille Lacs Band of Ojibwe. The band had sued the state in 1990, claiming the state was violating its hunting and fishing rights under an 1837 treaty with the US government.

Under the settlement, the state agreed to transfer fifteen thousand acres of land near the reservation and provide $8.6 million in a lump-sum payment to the band. The state also agreed to allow band members to net and spear game fish in a six-thousand-acre zone in the southwestern corner of Lake Mille Lacs and other lakes and rivers. In return, the band agreed to withdraw the lawsuit, limit walleye fish harvests to twenty-four thousand pounds a year, and practice conservation. I felt the agreement was reasonable. All treaties supersede state and federal law. Similar lawsuits in Michigan and Wisconsin had already established that these rights existed. Therefore the state needed to recognize the hunting and fishing rights held by this sovereign nation. The settlement was very controversial, however, with sportsmen who worried it would deplete the walleye supply and hurt tourism.[4]

The house's chief author on the bill to approve the agreement, DFL representative David Battaglia, believed he would be able to produce enough votes to pass the bill out of committee and onto the house floor. He asked me to be the Republican second author. We thought we'd just make it on the floor, though we knew the margin would be close. While most members of my Republican caucus were allied with the sportsmen, Battaglia was counting on some minority votes for passage.

When it came time to vote, several on each side didn't show their preference. The voting board stayed open.

Jim Wafler, the floor aide for house speaker Irv Anderson, came to me and said, "Where are your twelve Republican votes? You promised us twelve votes."

Nobody had asked me to count votes. I didn't know what Wafler was talking about.

He continued, "We're not going to put up all of our votes and have your members get away with the easy vote in opposition to the settlement. We're not going to put our members at risk. You need to put up your twelve votes, or the bill is going down."

I was still confused. "Where did you get the idea there would be twelve Republican votes?" I asked him.

"The aide from the governor's office told us."

Aides for Governor Arne Carlson worked the legislature to ensure his priorities were enacted into law, and the governor backed this settlement. I went off the floor and called his aide, Cindy Jepsen. I asked if she had promised twelve Republican votes to the majority for the bill.

"Well, I think there should be twelve votes," she said. "I looked over the list of new members in your caucus, and there should be at least that many in support."

She named a couple Republicans who she believed would

back the treaty. "Workman, Pawlenty, all of those freshmen should support it," she said.

But she hadn't spoken with any of them. I went to Tom Workman and Tim Pawlenty and several other Republican freshmen. All were surprised by my approach and told me they were voting no.

What a mess! The Democrats had presented the bill on the basis of the aide's promise that there would be at least twelve Republican votes. Now they thought we were trying to double-cross them. Time was running out to fix the misunderstanding. The vote was being taken, and it was clear there wouldn't be twelve Republicans in favor.

When Irv Anderson saw what was happening, he thought the Republicans were betraying an agreement. He switched his vote from supporting the treaty to opposing it.

Once his vote went up as no, or red, the Democrats who were taking the harder yes vote immediately switched. Without clear leadership and with fear of political fallout, many house members decided the safe vote was against the treaty settlement. The bill went down 64–70, four votes short of the bare majority needed to pass it.

Again, a good bill failed to pass the legislature because trust had collapsed. There had been poor communication and strategy from the governor's office. Only nine of forty-six Republicans voted for the bill, though the governor had heavily lobbied for and expected more. The governor's office didn't do the work needed to persuade individual members. Instead they acted as if the Republican legislators should just be expected to follow the governor's lead.[5]

As a result of the failure, the state entered a legal battle that ended up costing Minnesota millions of dollars. The dispute went all the way to the US Supreme Court, which ruled 5–4 in 1999 that the Mille Lacs band retained hunting and fishing rights guaranteed by the 1837 treaty.

Another repercussion was that Battaglia, the author of the treaty legislation, decided not to run for reelection. He thought he had been betrayed by the house speaker. In reality, Battaglia had been a victim of miscommunication resulting in distrust.

In both of these bills, maintaining the trust among legislators and between legislators and the public-interest groups was necessary to avoid the failure of a good idea. This is the really critical lesson for these cases.

CHAPTER 3

{ Power Sharing }

Majority control is a basic precept of our American governmental system. Yet majority control can also be a perversion of democracy, a form of tyranny, the tyranny of the majority. Taxation without representation is the best example of this kind of tyranny. When early American colonialists rebelled against England, it was because they were not represented within the British legislature. It definitely happens that majority control within a legislature can suppress the ideas and initiatives of the minority. This type of governance is more tyrannical than democratic. Democratically structured bicameral and bipartisan legislatures require power sharing by both minority and majority parties for effective representation of the public and enactment of laws.

Minority members make it easier for the majority to share power when they show support for and help the majority pass good nonpartisan bills. Unfortunately, the majority's committee chairs often use their gavel and their formal power to discourage any minority participation. If a partisan majority chair refuses a hearing for a minority member's nonpartisan bill, for example, the minority member must find creative ways like those described in this book to get the chair to change course and hold the hearing. Sometimes progress is made only after a minority member keeps working on a problem through multiple sessions, involving members of the majority when possible—until the majority is ready to accept a bill.

Persuasion is another form of power sharing. In a democracy, ordinary voters recognize persuasive consensus building as successful leadership. This is true not only in politics and government, but also in other social organizations. Churches, employment groups, teachers' unions, and lawyers' and doctors' groups all need to have leaders who persuade followers to work with them. Even industry is now emphasizing teamwork and group work, and employees are encouraged to come up with suggestions to improve the process.

Power sharing isn't just "Look, you help me and I'll help you," though the general public might think so. "You scratch my back, I'll scratch yours" is not bridge building because there is no common goal. There is very little that is accomplished like that, and for me, such arrangements were rare.

I saw excellent power sharing and teamwork in a 1994 Judiciary Finance Committee chaired by DFL representative Mary Murphy. While developing a bill, she involved all interested members and helped them to work together. She asked each of us to take a designated area of the bill and do some special screening of the financial requests. This process worked very well. The contrast with the senate bill when we got to the conference committee was obvious. Our bill was the result of broad bipartisan participation. In putting the bill on the table for all of us to work on, Representative Murphy demonstrated power sharing at its best.

A member's political-caucus identification also limits

another facet of legislating. As a minority member, I was not able to go directly to the majority caucus with a bill. Many times, the real future of a piece of legislation is decided in the majority caucus and not on the floor, leaving the minority unable to participate or make any arguments. Bridge building with majority members helped me get around this problem. If I could sell my bill in a committee early on, I knew the majority members from that committee could then advocate for the bill when it was discussed in their private caucus meeting. The committee members would have heard arguments on both sides of the issue and been prepared to argue for the bill during the caucus.

In the 1984 legislative session, DFL representative Randy Kelly asked me to coauthor his bill concerning filling vacancies in judicial offices. Often a chief author will find members who are willing to coauthor a bill. It is frequently a benefit to the bill to have influential coauthors because they add strength to the bill. On politically attractive bills, legislators are glad to be asked to coauthor because they get political credit for themselves.

In this case, Kelly wanted my help. Kelly's bill set up a committee on judicial vacancies composed of four members appointed by the governor and four members appointed by the chief justice of the Minnesota Supreme Court. In addition, one attorney and one judge from the district where the vacancy occurred would sit with the committee and send the governor the names of the three most qualified applicants. The governor would be required to appoint one of these three or send the committee a request for another three candidates.[1]

At the time, most judges had been appointed by the governor to fill a vacancy after a sitting judge had resigned or died before the end of his or her elective term. This meant that historically, judicial appointments were very political. Kelly's proposal to have a committee make recommendations based on merit appeared to be a much preferable method.

As Kelly and I discussed the legislation, I mentioned that an election was coming up in the fall.

"You mean we might lose our majority power?" Kelly said with a laugh. "No way."

Well, that outcome is precisely what happened. The house majority's leader, Speaker Harry Sieben, retired from the legislature to resume his law practice. This sparked a myopic approach to leadership succession by several potential speakers who focused more on lining up caucus supporters than on the general election. So in 1984, the Republicans took control of the state house for the first time in fourteen years. The turnover was also a result of vigorous work finding new Republican candidates, done by Representatives David Jennings, Steve Sviggum, Cal Ludeman, and Ray Welker. This upset was a surprise to both caucuses.

Kelly had been unable to pass his judicial merit selection bill in the 1984 session. When the 1985 session got underway, Kelly had become a minority member without the power of the gavel. He again brought his bill to me. But this time he wanted me, now in the majority, to be chief author.

"You keep it," I told him. "It's your idea and your work. I'll help as coauthor again."

I went to the new Republican chairman of the house Judiciary Committee, Representative Chuck Halberg, and asked him to respect Kelly's originality and give him a hearing on his bill. The chairman agreed. Kelly persuaded the committee to recommend it to pass. The bill was successful in the house and senate, and then Kelly got Governor Perpich to sign it. Our willingness to share power meant that a good idea became law.

My time serving in the majority party didn't last long. The Democrats regained the majority in the 1986 election in spite of our Republican majority's success in cutting a billion dollars out of the $11 billion budget for the 1985–86 biennium. The Democratic caucus got its act together and won the '86 election, fueled by the popular Governor Perpich's reelection.

Now in the majority again, Kelly and his colleagues didn't forget my helpfulness when they had been in the minority. Representative (and later senator, and then mayor of St. Paul) Kelly remained a friend and occasional ally. He became chairman of the Judiciary Committee and gave me many hearings over several years, and he was the only DFL senator to help with our community notification bill. We had successfully begun a habit of power sharing. This sharing was beneficial to me because the house Democrats remained in power for the next twelve years.

The best example of power sharing I ever saw in my twenty-year legislative career occurred in 1989. That year, the legislature enacted what would quickly become regarded as a landmark law, the Minnesota Groundwater Protection Act.

What led me into this legislation was a problem in my own county. My friend and county commissioner Jean Michaels asked me to come to a meeting on groundwater pollution at the county administrator's office. The county's growing numbers of private septic systems were leaking through the porous karst geology and into the groundwater supply, and the landfill was potentially leaking as well. I picked up the phone right then and called Representative Willard Munger at his home in Duluth. Munger's specialty, as I've mentioned previously, was environmental protection. I told him we had a groundwater pollution problem, and he interrupted me and told me he was working on a bill right then for groundwater protection—and that I was going to be one of the authors. Here was the bridge again.

Munger and his assistant, Ann Glumac, structured his bill into several defined areas for groundwater protection and decided to apportion responsibility among five legislators, three Democrats and two Republicans. They carefully chose coauthors who could work with different interest groups whose support was necessary for the bill to gain passage. For instance, Representative Henry Kalis, a DFL grain farmer, and Representative Elton Redalen, a Republican dairy farmer, stood for the state's two most important agricultural interests.

DFL representative Len Price and I worked with the state's Pollution Control Agency. Price focused on the issue of where new wells could be located while I directed my focus to how abandoned groundwater wells would be identified and handled.

At committee hearings, two or more of these coauthors would often explain different aspects of the bill, while Munger brought his personal leadership and credibility to the forefront in overseeing the overall bill.

The result was a groundwater protection act that had several innovative provisions. It was the first act in the country to reimburse farmers for the costs they incurred to clean up agricultural chemical spills. It also provided partial funding of groundwater protection programs by using a "polluter pay" surcharge fee, applied to agricultural chemicals and applicators so that those who use the polluting materials help pay for the cleanup.[2]

This was an example of successful legislation that had broad bipartisan support and power sharing. It became a national model and received an award for innovation from the Center for Policy Alternatives, a Washington think tank, which gave credit to and named all five authors. It wasn't called a power-sharing award, but that is what I would have dubbed it. This was group work at its finest.[3]

CASE: Sexual-Predator Politics

In July 1987, while I was in the minority, some of my majority colleagues undertook a repeal of the state's 1939 psychopathic-personality statute, Minnesota Chapter 526. The statute had been used to send sex offenders to treatment facilities instead of prison. The constitutionality of the statute had been successfully defended, but it had lost its meaning over the years. Dr. Lee Beecher, president of the Minnesota Psychiatric Association, had approached my house colleagues Representatives Lee Greenfield and Kathleen Vellenga about changing the law. He told them the term "psychopathic personality" was no longer recognized as a professionally appropriate diagnosis. Recent reports had found no reliable data demonstrating the effectiveness of treatment, and, consequently, many states were either repealing their sexual-psychopath statutes or modifying them. As there was no known cure or effective treatment for these people, the Psychiatric Association felt they should be kept in correctional facilities.[4]

The psychiatrists also didn't like the idea of using the Minnesota Security Hospital, which was designed for the mentally ill and dangerous, to house sexual psychopaths. The Department of Human Services had become responsible for the treatment and the confinement of these individuals, who, though dangerous, were not mentally ill.

Many of them had been directly committed as psychopathic personalities from a civil proceeding without being charged or tried in a criminal court, however, and without a criminal conviction, they could not be held in prison. And even though the total number of these persons was a small percentage of all sex offenders, they were a clearly defined group and were very dangerous and likely to repeat their crimes.[5]

I wanted to get involved with Greenfield and Vellenga's effort. While in private law practice, I had represented a man who had raped and tried to kill a woman. He was sentenced to prison and served eight years of the thirty-year sentence. After his release he raped again. That time he was civilly committed to the Minnesota Security Hospital as a psychopathic personality. So I knew firsthand what the risks were, and wanted to help find a way to avoid them.

The commissioner of health appointed a task force to examine issues related to the Minnesota Commitment Act. I was part of it, and my subcommittee was charged with reviewing issues related to Chapter 526.[6]

Dr. Beecher, who was also on the task force, argued that people committed under this law should have been housed in prisons, but that seemed too simplistic to me. He didn't seem to realize that many of these people had never actually been convicted of a crime. If the statute were repealed without any alternative legislation, the decision would create a loophole allowing for the release of about seventy very dangerous persons.

Task force members debated vigorously as to whether sexual psychopaths should be housed in prisons or state hospitals. But in considering the repeal of Chapter 526, safety to the public seemed clearly the most important issue. So I sided with four task force colleagues, including Judge Lindsay Arthur and Department of Corrections commissioner Orville Pung, to keep the law as it was, allowing hospitalization of the offenders. There were problems with the statute, but I didn't feel repealing it was the right thing to do. Dr. Beecher, Representatives Greenfield and Vellenga, and some other professionals in the field voted to repeal the statute, meaning the imprisoned offenders would be released. We deadlocked on a 5–5 vote, so no recommendation came out of the task force.

And nothing happened in the legislature on the issue for five years.

Though the legislature stayed on the sidelines, I was still worried that the 1939 law was at risk, so I stayed active in this area. In 1988 I was appointed to the eighteen-member task force on the prevention of sexual violence against women created by Attorney General Skip Humphrey. Our task force proposed tougher sentences for rapists and other sex offenders. As it was, few convicts spent enough time in jail to complete chemical-dependence and sexual-violence treatment programs.[7]

In 1991, commissioner of Human Services Natalie Steffen organized a planning team between her agency and the Department of Corrections to look at psychopath commitments. It called for action to change the vagueness of the old law and for a comprehensive law which would meet the needs of the current situation. The Minnesota Psychiatric Society distributed a report in 1992 that laid out some very specific recommendations for how to fix the psychopathic-personality problems. I met with Steffen and began reading all I could find on the subject of sexual predators.[8]

In 1993, the subject became urgent. There was a case challenging the law before the state supreme court. The petitioner was Phillip Blodgett, a young man who had a long history of sexual misconduct and violence and had been committed to the Minnesota Security Hospital as a psychopathic personality. Blodgett's case claimed Chapter 526 was unconstitutional because it violated substantive due process and was in violation of the equal-protection guarantee of the federal and Minnesota constitutions. The case was argued in May of that year, and as of November the court still hadn't announced a decision.[9]

I was afraid once more that the supreme court might throw out the statute and many dangerous sex offenders would be released. To me this case meant the legislature couldn't wait any longer to act.

I reached out to Emily Shapiro in house research to search for sex-offender solutions in other states. She found a statute from Washington State that had been passed in 1990. We put together a bill modeled after the Washington law and made it ready for introduction in the 1994 session. I asked house majority leader Phil Carruthers to be a coauthor because I wanted the Democratic leadership on board. The chairman of our task force, Representative Wes Skoglund—also the chairman of the house Judiciary Committee—was another coauthor.

The day I was planning to introduce the bill, I got a phone call from John Hughes, a reporter for the *Rochester Post-Bulletin*. "I don't think you'll need the bill," Hughes said. "The supreme court just decided 4–3 to uphold the psychopathic-personality statute."[10]

But while my bill was no longer urgently needed, I decided to continue working on it. I was still concerned that the law was in jeopardy. Working with representatives of the Minnesota County Attorneys Association and the attorney general's office, I managed to get the bill approved in the full house. However, my effort to get a senate companion bill was opposed by Allan Spear, chairman of the senate Crime Prevention and Public Safety Committee. Spear was a strong civil libertarian who thought the offenders were entitled to exactly the same liberties as anybody else. When my proposal went to a conference committee as part of the omnibus crime bill, senate conferees led by Spear opposed the house language.[11]

In March, at one of the conference-committee meetings, I decided to go off to the side and write a possible compromise. My provision called for the establishment of a new legislative task force to examine the current law and practices relating to the commitment of psychopathic personalities and make recommendations on options, both civil and criminal, for dealing with sexual predators. The task force consisted of people from the attorney general's office and officials from the Departments of Corrections and Human Services. This adjustment was acceptable to Spear and the other senators.[12]

In June 1994, after the legislature had adjourned, the Minnesota Supreme Court decided two other cases that resulted in two convicted sex offenders, Dennis Linehan and Peter Rickmyer, being released to halfway houses. I got a call from the sister of a woman whom Linehan had raped. She lived in Rochester and told me the rapist had threatened their family when he was sentenced, saying to her sister that he would find her once he got out. This strengthened my belief that the legislature needed to take action to ensure that more dangerous predators would not get released.

The task force began meeting that summer. The matter had become urgent once again. Not only had Linehan and Rickmyer been released, but seven more petitions had been filed and many more were expected. Unlike the previous task force that had deadlocked, our group this time decided Minnesota needed to have a revised statute to address the sexual-predator threat. The task force met thirteen times to gather information and get input from many professionals familiar with the statute. It held over forty-four hours of testimony.[13]

Our task force visited the Minnesota Security Hospital, where sex offenders were being treated. We were told by the director that the new wording in our bill for sexual predators, and its new three-part formula for identifying them, were significant improvements over existing law. With this definition, we used the term "sexually dangerous person" to describe someone who has engaged in a course of harmful sexual conduct, has manifested a sexual personality rather than a mental disorder or dysfunction, and, as a result of both, is likely to engage in future acts of harmful sexual conduct. The formula and its verbal standards were sufficiently objective to justify continuing to keep the most dangerous offenders in a state hospital, where they could be treated for the disorder.

The task force's recommendations, along with the two high-profile cases, really got things moving. The mood of the Minnesota public had also changed. There had been several recent cases of abductions, rapes, and murders of children, and the voters wanted tougher laws. Further, we were heading into an election cycle where the voters would want to see their legislators proving themselves to be tough on crime.

We revised my bill, adding due-process clauses, but still used the Washington State statute as a model, as well as a Kansas statute. Both laws had been heard and affirmed by the US Supreme Court. My bill used the three-part formula to define mental disorders for persons unable to resist their sexual impulses and wrongful behavior. The formula and its verbal standards were sufficiently objective to justify continuing to keep the most dangerous offenders in a state hospital, where they could be treated for the disorder.

The governor called a special session for August 31 for the purpose of consideration and passage of this single piece of legislation. Representative Skoglund stepped forward to take chief authorship of the bill. He got house rules suspended to allow for immediate consideration, and we both worked our caucuses privately to keep politically tasty amendments from messing up the bill. Skoglund and I each explained the bill on the floor.[14]

In less than four hours, the bill was passed 65–0 in the senate and 133–0 in the house and signed by Governor Arne Carlson, taking effect immediately. Collaboration between Skoglund and me resulted in a bipartisan solution that everyone agreed with. The legislature had acted unanimously because of this power sharing. Within the next twenty-four hours, Linehan and Rickmyer were recommitted to the state hospital. The enforcement of this legislation would bring its own issues for subsequent legislators to address, but for the time being, we had solved the problem.[15]

CASE: Community-Notification Struggle

In summer 1994, while I was working on the sexual-predator bill, I received a call from a probation officer at the prison in Stillwater. He knew I was looking at the Washington State sexual-predator law as a model for Minnesota and suggested I examine closely its community-notification provision. This officer had a frustrating experience: when a woman called his office and asked the whereabouts of a released sex offender, he had to say that by law he could not tell her anything. He felt the public needed a community-notification law that would allow authorities to release information about which sex offenders were living in various neighborhoods.

I was intrigued, so I brought the concept of requiring community notification to the task force. We heard some testimony on the idea, and the media began to pick up on it. But thc timing wasn't right. We had nearly finished our work on the sexual-predator bill, and it would be ready for the 1994 special session. We didn't want to bog it down with a new idea that would require much testimony and work. In 1995, however, I prepared a community-notification bill for introduction. Like the Washington State law, my bill simply authorized law enforcement to release sex-offender registration information when necessary to protect the public. At the time, New Jersey was working on its own version of community notification, called "Megan's Law." I talked with some people in that state's attorney general's office, but I wasn't comfortable with their method of turning over the assessment and notification decisions to prosecutors. This seemed to be a step in the direction of punishment, which could tip the balance away from a civil regulation toward a criminal action and move into the dangerous constitutional ground of double jeopardy.

While creating the bill, I had called several people in Washington State to find out how the law was working. One key contact was Roxanne Lieb at the Washington State Institute for Public Policy, who had studied the law's implementation. Her work helped define areas where Minnesota's law would need to improve upon the one in Washington. For example, Washington's law gave each county's and city's law enforcement authority to develop risk assessments and guidelines for notification. Officials in cities like Seattle had put a lot of thought into the process, but other cities didn't even have written policies. There wasn't much conformity across the state.

Another key contact was Ernie Allen, president of the

National Center for Missing and Exploited Children. Allen came to Minnesota early in the 1995 session and testified in support of my bill. He was joined by Patty Wetterling, a Minnesota woman whose son Jacob had been abducted in the previous decade. Wetterling was a powerful advocate on issues surrounding missing children. Allen and Wetterling's testimony helped build support for the bill and brought media attention to the idea.

I worked closely with Representative Wes Skoglund. We started talking to some key players in our state, including some detectives from the Minneapolis Police Department's sex-crimes unit. They were concerned about bearing responsibility for risk assessment which would be used to determine whether an offender's deeds had been serious enough to warrant community notification. They were particularly worried about how they would conduct the work without additional funding. And the police weren't alone in wanting to avoid more responsibilities. The county attorneys were worried about the New Jersey model and told me they didn't want any role in the process; the Department of Corrections did not want to do the risk assessments; the sheriffs were worried about having responsibility for notifications.

Working with all of these groups, I drafted a new bill that specified a three-tiered risk assessment that would be administered statewide by the Department of Corrections. The bill also specified where and to whom the information would be disclosed, depending on the risk level of the offender. Most importantly, we included a process for judicial review of the offender's assessed risk. I was anticipating court decisions similar to those already occurring in New Jersey, focused on due process, and I wanted to avoid similar problems in our law.

Despite the progress, I had difficulty finding a senate author for the bill. I went to at least five different senators and asked them to take a look and support it. No one wanted to take it on. All expressed some discomfort with the idea. They checked with Allan Spear, the senate Judiciary Committee chairman, and were told they were unlikely to get a hearing.

Over in the house, the bill had two hearings in the Judiciary Committee. It was approved and referred to the Judiciary Finance Committee. There was surprisingly little debate, probably because most house members knew that the bill was completely stalled in the senate. It was a safe vote for a popular, but potentially controversial, proposal that looked like it would never make it in the 1995 session.

At this point, the Department of Corrections caused me some irritation by supplying an estimated cost for the bill that I felt was exaggerated. I knew that they didn't like the new responsibilities they were being given, and the expensive fiscal note was one weapon they could use to sink the bill. I debated many of their assumptions. In the end, the Judiciary Finance Committee allocated a small amount of funding in the 1995 omnibus crime bill, which was eventually passed by the full house.

I still couldn't find an author in the senate.

One night, I went to supper with Randy Kelly, now a senator, and mentioned community notification. "I need help," I said. "This is a popular idea and I know the people want it. I don't want to make a partisan issue of it, but when we pass something through the house and can't get anywhere in the senate, it looks like the senate's Democrats are blocking it. You should at least take a look at it."

I knew I could bring this up with Kelly because I had helped him in the past, as I've mentioned. We had served for eight years together in the house, and had a reciprocal relationship that went back to 1984, when we worked together on the bill dealing with merit selection of judges. I knew Kelly had guts. When he thought something was a good idea and the right thing to do, he'd stick his neck out. He wasn't intimidated by the opposition of other senators.

Kelly reviewed the bill and agreed to author it.

All the stars had finally aligned, but the proposal did not receive a hearing in the senate that year. Supposedly this was because Kelly signed on too late in the session. I was frustrated. How were we going to overcome the opposition in the senate? The obvious first step was to publicly lay the blame for the bill's failure on the senate, implying that the senators were more worried about sex offenders' rights than the public's right to protect its children. This step had to be done with some finesse because I didn't want to make senators mad. However, it was an easy task to remind the media where the bill had stalled.

At the house-senate conference committee on judiciary finance, I made a point of telling senators that the community-notification bill would not go away.

"This bill will pass in 1996, when the entire senate is up for reelection," I said.

I left the conference committee with an agreement to set up a further "work group" to study community notification.

It was called a work group, not a task force, at Spear's insistence: he thought "task force" was too suggestive that something needed to be accomplished.

But several things happened over summer and autumn 1995 to soften Spear's opposition. First, public support for the bill grew. The Jacob Wetterling Foundation hired a full-time legislative consultant, Julie Henderson, to work on the bill. Henderson began visiting neighborhood meetings to educate people and build a base of support, focusing on the districts of those senators who opposed the bill. The foundation also publicized the bill to its many supporters. Patty Wetterling appeared as a witness before our work group.

The second key event was Bob Shilling's appearance before the work group in October 1995. Shilling, a detective with the Seattle Police Department, was in charge of administering the city's community-notification program. Shilling explained how Seattle used community meetings not just to inform the public about a sex offender's release but also to defuse anger and educate parents. He showed us the types of bulletins police posted and discussed how his department had refined the type of information they released to minimize the community's fear.

Shilling's testimony made community notification seem workable. Opponents had constantly brought up the specter of vigilantism, but Shilling was able to show that a controlled response and extensive community education had eliminated incidents of harassment.

Up until Shilling's visit, the work group had been meeting and reviewing other states' laws but hadn't done much substantial work. I knew that a turning point had come when

Marcia Greenfield, Senator Spear's assistant, was heard after the meeting to say, "Am I crazy, or does this actually sound like it could work?"

Sometime after the meeting, the senate DFL caucus released an agenda for the upcoming 1996 session. Community notification was listed as a priority. Spear's mind had changed.

The house DFL caucus also decided to make the issue a priority for the next session. Once both caucuses had publicly adopted the issue, it wouldn't make sense from their point of view to leave me, a Republican, as the chief author. The idea was popular, and it had never been identified as a Republican issue, so it would be easy for them to take it away from me.

Representative Skoglund had been the chairman of our work group, and when it came time to produce a product, he had a new bill drawn up that included most of the group's recommendations. He used my bill, with minor amendments, as the structure for the proposal, but he was the lone author of the new piece of legislation. I had always been suspicious that Representative Skoglund wanted to take over the bill in the house, but I'd never had any direct evidence. It was becoming clear I was being left out of the process. I faced a dilemma. I knew there was still more work to be done on the bill, but if I wanted to be involved, I was going to have to do it on Skoglund's bill and let him take the credit.

Kelly, the senate author, stepped in and gave me an alternative. He told me his bill was the lead item on the senate's crime-prevention agenda. He said his proposal would continue to move as the companion to the bill I had introduced in the house in 1995 (which automatically carried forward into the second year of the biennium), not to Skoglund's new bill. Kelly got Senator Spear to agree to the approach.

Kelly arranged a meeting in the senate offices with Representative Lee Greenfield, senate counsel Ken Backus, Senator Don Betzold, and me. We came up with a new method for assessing the risk a released sex offender would pose, focusing more on the prediction of future dangerousness rather than on past criminal history. This change greatly reduced costs for the Department of Corrections. The language on the information that would be disclosed was also refined. We used the most recent New Jersey Supreme Court decision as our guide. These changes seemed to make Senator Betzold, who had been skeptical about the bill, more comfortable.

Kelly invited me to sit next to him at the witness table when his bill had its first senate hearing. It was unusual to have a member of the other body, and the other caucus, present information and answer questions.

It was at this first senate hearing that the county attorneys surfaced. Dick Armey, from Washington County, wrote a letter opposing the bill. The county attorneys were worried about defending the risk-assessment decision during a judicial-review hearing. They must have realized that the train had already left the station, however, because instead of attacking the specifics of the bill directly, they tried to argue that the only state action necessary was to make registration files public. I was angry about this because I don't like being opposed by surprise, and the county attorneys were quite influential.

I called Ray Schmitz, an Olmsted County attorney who

had served on the work group and had never given me any indication that the county attorneys opposed community notification. He had an idea for a different level of judicial review, so I scheduled another phone conference with Schmitz and had my criminal-law expert from house research, Emily Shapiro, join us as we worked out the details. Schmitz proposed that administrative-law judges review these cases. An administrative-law judge is a government official who is not part of the judicial branch and who presides at administrative hearings to resolve disputes between a government agency and someone affected by a decision or action of that agency. Decisions made by such judges are final but are usually subject to review by an appellate judicial court. For us, Schmitz's suggestion was a less expensive and simpler alternative to formal judicial review that would still protect the offender's due-process rights. This would limit the involvement of both the county attorneys and the courts, keeping costs down. It was an alternative that I could sell. Shapiro and I were excited by the idea, and she went to work drafting the language.

Another important change that came out of the conversation with Schmitz was to limit the scope of the administrative review. We had originally thought that the actual notification decision made by law enforcement should be subject to administrative review, but on further thought, this approach seemed unworkable. Offenders would be able to challenge every decision made by law enforcement and tie up the process indefinitely.

Next, I called on John Stuart, the state public defender. I knew that Senators Spear and Betzold, and Republican senator Tom Neuville, all of whom had various levels of concern about the bill, would listen to Stuart. They trusted his judgment. Stuart, though he may have been philosophically opposed to the idea, didn't speak against the bill. It was unrealistic for him to advocate for the idea, yet his silence sent a clear message to skeptical senators. Though he had concerns, he knew he needed to find a realistic way to involve the public defenders. He worked out a reasonable staffing level for the predicted workload, and I included funding for that in the bill.

Now I had to sell the proposed changes to Senator Kelly. I met with him and his staff several times. Kelly was confident, however, that he could pass the bill in its current form in the senate, despite the objections of the county attorneys. He told me the new ideas looked like problems and that the best strategy was to move the existing bill.

With Kelly's reluctance to adopt the changes, I knew I had to find a way to make the alterations in the house instead. The problem, of course, was that I was no longer chief author of the house bill. I didn't want to hand all of my work over to Representative Skoglund, but I also felt strongly that the changes I had worked out to satisfy the county attorneys were needed. While I was still struggling over how to handle this dilemma, I organized a meeting with Shapiro, Bill Guelker from the Department of Corrections, and other interested parties to continue fine-tuning my newest draft. Even though my draft was an orphan, I wanted to continue working out the details so it would be ready when an opportunity arose.

Then, just by chance, I ran into Skoglund's committee administrator, Greg Bergstrom. In one moment, I decided to invite Skoglund to the meeting. It was a turning point. Skoglund agreed to attend.

When the meeting was convened, Skoglund listened to me go over my changes for the house bill. I explained how they would satisfy the objections of the county attorneys— which I had become convinced constituted a valid point. It was more important that a good bill be enacted than that I get credit for it. Joining forces with Wes Skoglund was the best way to do this. After our meeting, Skoglund changed his own bill, incorporating Ray Schmitz's suggestion.

When it came time to present the new product to the house Judiciary Committee, Skoglund invited me to present his bill with him. Skoglund's willingness to collaborate persuaded me to change direction and support his amended bill instead of mine. This was power sharing going both ways. The teamwork strengthened the bill and put it in a better position for passage by the legislature. As a majority party committee chair, Skoglund was open to participation by a minority member that would strengthen the bill. The committee unanimously passed the bill. It then went to the house floor, where it was also approved. Finally, community notification went to a successful conference committee and was signed into law by Governor Arne Carlson.

Clearly, the community notification proposal took a long, twisted path to success. The key to getting it done was that, over the years, I carefully formed a coalition of all parties who would be involved and then met their concerns, slowly and fully. The final element was the inclusion of Representative Skoglund. Again bipartisan bridge building paved the way for legislation that served the public good.

CHAPTER 4

The Power of the Conference Committee

While power sharing is important for success, a legislator must always remember that his job is to represent the interests of his constituents. It is expected that a strong representative will be willing to play hardball, and there is one place where a legislator can have significant influence: the conference committee. "Conference committee" has a specific meaning for legislatures, but the action of this committee is similar to that in many organizations where a plurality of ideas and goals needs to be pounded out into one cohesive proposal. The search for common ground is especially important here.

I learned about conference committees shortly after I was first elected and moved into my office across the hall from a Republican legislator, Merlyn Valan. New legislators often find more senior members intimidating. I didn't. I always felt that since more experienced persons knew the ropes, they could be helpful. Valan was an example of this.

One day, Valan asked me over for coffee in his office. He had an open, friendly nature. "Dave, you're a retired lawyer and financially independent with enough income to enjoy life. Why are you here? What do you want to do?"

"Merlyn," I said, "I like law, and I want the opportunity to make good law." I told him that, as a novice legislator, I was perplexed about how the system worked and what freshman legislators were supposed to do.

Valan then told me, "The way to make law up here is to get on conference committees. The final draft of any piece of legislation that comes out of both the house and senate is put together by a conference committee. That's where the real power is." Conference committees are made up of members from both houses, and they resolve the differences between the versions of a bill that each house has passed.

"Well, how would I get on conference committees?" I asked.

"The way you get on a conference committee is to be nominated by the chief author of the bill," Valan said. "The chief author is asked by the house speaker to give a list of names for the committee. It will either be three names for minor bills or five names for major bills. There will almost always be a minority member on the committee if any minority members voted for the bill." I was lapping up every word of Valan's lecture.

"The author wants to have people on the conference committee who not only are in favor of the bill, but have helped it," Valan continued. "So if you see a need for an amendment, you go to the chief author, talk to him about his bill, and tell him you could support it. Then you might suggest your amendment. If you end up helping the bill, the author is going to want you on the conference committee."

I took the lesson to heart and swiftly put it into practice. I spoke with bill authors, offered amendments, and was a source of support for legislation when I thought the basic purpose was good. I used Valan's lesson in every legislative session of my career. As a minority legislator, this was the role I chose.

In my first year in office, out of forty-two freshman legislators, I requested to be and fortunately was put on the Appropriations Committee. I was on the state departments division, which covered funding for most of the state agencies. DFL representative Phyllis Kahn was chairwoman. She was bright, informed, and tenacious. I was often a positive force on her committee and so she included me in almost every session after that—ultimately I served on the division for sixteen years.

My first experience on a conference committee was in 1983. The committee was led by veteran DFL representative Wayne Simoneau. For one stretch, our panel was dealing with a new pay schedule for state employees. When the work was nearly done, the chairman asked, "Is there anything else?"

"Well, Mr. Chair," I said, "I see the house bill has district judges' pay set at forty-six thousand dollars, and the senate has it at forty-seven thousand dollars. So I propose we compromise at forty-eight thousand dollars." After the laughter ended, committee members saw both my humor and that I was actually serious. I wanted to use my conference-committee power to get judges better pay. The bill passed with my fix.

On conference committees, negotiation is a form of partnering because legislators have to bring themselves and others together, at least for a moment. They have to share information and build trust. They also need to understand exactly what each side really wants and on which policy positions they can give leeway. The goal is to get a win-win, and this may involve adopting positions from either of the two bill sources, the house and the senate. The challenge of conference-committee work is in trying to negotiate between the house bill and the senate bill to put together a package where each side gets some of what they want. It's important for each side to make concessions on what is going into the bill. The age-old Roman phrase *quid pro quo* means *one thing in return for another* or "this for that" (in Latin).

In a bonding-bill conference committee I served on in 1987, there were two or three items proposed that would benefit Duluth. Sam Solon in the senate and Willard Munger in the house, both Democrats from Duluth, were on that committee. They were both known for playing a fine game of hardball within their caucuses, and had a reputation for using seniority and power to get funds for state projects in their city. One day, the committee chair called a meeting without including Solon and Munger and announced that the committee would not take up any Duluth issues until the end of the committee's work. Dealing with these items up front would put Solon and Munger in better negotiating positions. They would be able to block parts of the conference committee's bill that other conferees sought. No one lost anything through this maneuver: our plan ended up working out for everyone, including Munger and Solon, by dealing with Duluth items last.

That day in 1983 when I went across the hall for coffee paid off repeatedly during my career. Valan's advice helped me accomplish quite a few things. DFL representative Rick

Krueger once told me that I, a minority member, had been requested by house chief authors for more conference committees than any other legislator with whom I served. Learning the ins and outs of conference committees and how to get appointed to them was far and away my most important lesson for success as a legislator.

CASE: A Bonding Maneuver

The most extraordinary conference committee I served on was for the 1995 bonding bill.

The legislation was called the bonding bill because it authorized the issuance of bonds to finance capital projects for the state. Traditionally, a bonding bill is passed every other year to fund construction of state buildings and renovate and repair structures as needed. It would be a poor decision on the part of the state to make taxpayers use that year's taxes to pay for long-term projects and building improvements. Projects are proposed in the senate and house capital-investment committees. A special provision in the state constitution requires that any bonding bill be approved by 60 percent of the members of each house before it can go to a conference committee. For the house, this requirement means eighty-one votes. Because house majorities in Minnesota have rarely been very lopsided, the party in control always has to get some votes from the minority in order to reach the cutoff. This necessitates sharing power in a collaborative manner.

Bonding bills often have trouble because they are so big—well into the hundreds of millions of dollars. The public perceives this as *new* spending, although the monies are not expended until projects are found ready for bids, usually years after the bills are enacted.

After the bills are approved by the required votes, the package of twenty-year bonds is sold in the bond market. Written state guidelines require that 40 percent of the bond's principal be repaid within the first five years, another 30 percent in the second five years, and the last 30 percent in the last ten years. These fast repayment requirements and low interest rates compare favorably with commercial and homeowners' mortgages. In addition, the total debt service—the total annual cost of principal plus interest—on the total outstanding bonds is limited based on a calculation of percent of state personal income. This guarantees a reasonable level of debt.[1]

These very conservative limits on the state twenty-year bonds have been poorly explained to the public. Many legislators are more concerned that the bond numbers look like a big new spending bill—an idea the media promotes. But bonding bills provide essential financing for building maintenance, roof repairs, and similar items that involve taking care of property owned by the state's people.

In 1995, majority Democrats failed three times to get enough Republican votes to pass the bonding bill. We house Republicans wouldn't supply the votes unless Democrats negotiated with us, and the Democrats' attitude was "We're going to do it our way."

When the regular session ended with an impasse on the bonding bill, Governor Arne Carlson called a special session. The bonding bill was one of three items to be addressed.

The extra time to legislate was a benefit for me because

I needed to add something to the bonding bill that I hadn't managed to get done during the regular session. A prior legislative session had approved $1.2 million in state planning funds for construction of the Rochester University Center, which would combine a portion of Winona State University with the Riverland Technical and Community College. But work could not be started until another legislature authorized the release of the funds. My session priority was to obtain this authorization.

I knew I would need to get the minority Republican seat on the bonding-bill conference committee.

I had examined the house floor votes during the regular session and determined that support from one more Republican and me would be enough for passage. Then Don Frerichs, another Rochester representative and my longtime friend, happened to drop by. I explained to Don that I needed to lock down one more Republican vote.

"You can count on me," Frerichs said.

I then went to see Steve Sviggum, the house Republican majority leader, and told him I had the extra votes, mine and Frerichs's, that would guarantee the bonding bill's passage. I asked him for our caucus seat on the conference committee.

"We've got to have a strong position on the bonding bill," I told Sviggum. "I won't get anything for myself at the expense of anyone else."

Sviggum listened and informed me that he had something he needed from the bonding bill, too. He said it was important for our caucus's conferee to help Republican representative Ken Wolf get language removed from the senate version of the bill that would affect his district.

"Ken has talked to me about it," I said. "I will protect his position."

There was one last hitch. Sviggum said he'd already designated Representative Jerry Dempsey, who had been the caucus lead on the capital-investment committee. But Dempsey had a lot less experience negotiating on conference committees than I did, and Sviggum trusted me to get what the caucus needed.

"I'll make the change," Sviggum said.

This was to be an unusual conference panel because while the senate had passed a bonding bill, no such legislation had been approved in the house. In fact, for that reason, it was not technically a conference committee. All work was done under special orders, which were issued by the house Rules Committee. This was the house capital investment bill that did not get enough votes to pass but was the best the house had to take to the bonding conference. We house Republicans would be defending positions, but not an actual bill.

As the conferees began work, we quickly got into conflict over the senate position on Wolf's issue. The Department of Natural Resources wanted money in the bonding bill to purchase lands around Eagle Creek in Savage, Minnesota, to protect a trout stream. Wolf and the city wanted some land adjacent to the stream left available for commercial and residential development. The city predicted a 25 percent reduction in its potential tax base if the state purchased all the land. We Republicans wanted to keep the DNR's dollar allocation low enough in the bonding bill that the agency wouldn't be able to purchase all the land it wanted.

Eagle Creek was a tough natural-resources issue to begin

with, but it was also heavily politicized by the environmentalists on the senate side. They were intense and not very candid. Resolving the Rochester University Center issue was also tricky. Republican Rochester senator Sheila Kiscaden had negotiated bonding-bill language at the last minute with Democratic senator and Finance chairman Gene Merriam that would release the planning money for the project. However, such a provision had of course not been approved by any committee in the house.

We faced vigorous opposition from John Ostrom, a senior staff member of the higher-education system. He felt we were making an end run around the normal process. That was because legislators typically only chose to fund the top priorities recommended by higher-education leaders in a bonding bill. I didn't think that we needed to follow that route. For me, it got down to the question of whether final authority for funding decisions should be made by the state bureaucracy or by the legislature, and I've always argued that legislators should decide.

A fellow house conferee was also skeptical about the Rochester project, and my role on the panel. "How did you get yourself on this committee?" DFL representative Tony Kinkel, chairman of the Higher Education Finance Committee, asked me in a handwritten note. "And how are you proposing to get something done that my committee absolutely stopped dead?"

I knew that DFL representatives Gene Pelowski of Winona and John Dorn of Mankato were on Kinkel's finance committee and had represented Winona State University and Mankato State University. Both universities were concerned that more money for Rochester's facility would increase competition with their campuses, so they regularly opposed us.

"As far as I'm concerned," Kinkel later told me, "this is the most fantastic example of political leapfrog I've ever seen."

I said to Kinkel, "This needs your attention, and I'd like to have you look it over to see what you can live with. Your approval is going to be needed if we're going to include it in the bill."

Kinkel cooled off a little and agreed to look it over. He then met with two of Rochester's higher-education lobbyists, Penny Reynen and Jerry Seck, to discuss their concerns. They met in Senator Merriam's office and rewrote the senate language until they came up with something we could all tolerate.

When the conference committee held its next meeting, I moved to accept the senate language on Rochester. The senators voted "no" on the language that they had just crafted!

Reynen was dumbfounded. The "no" vote didn't bother me, however, because I knew what the senators were up to. I told her their vote was part of a familiar strategy on conference committees. The senators didn't want to agree to the Rochester language early in the process or I would have been free to swing hard at whatever else they wanted.

"Stay cool," I told her. "This is poker."

The conference committee continued its business and worked through nearly all the remaining issues. When we got down to the last few and the senators were trying to finish the committee's business, I decided to play my cards.

Senator Randy Kelly made a motion to accept the house

position on a certain uncontroversial construction project. I don't even remember what it was, but everyone on both sides of the table understood the project to be worthwhile. House Democrats on the conference committee raised their hands in favor of the project. I didn't. My house colleagues looked at me. "No," I said, and shook my head.

DFL representative Loren Solberg, sitting next to me, took his hand down and said, "No." One by one, the other house Democrats did the same.

"I don't understand what's going on," Senator Kelly said. "The senate has moved the house position."

"Senator Kelly," Solberg said, "what you don't understand is that the house will not have the votes for a bonding bill unless it has Representative Bishop's support. He controls the Republican votes necessary to pass the bill."

I had signaled it was time to reach an agreement on sticky issues, or no bonding bill would go forward. Committee business then quickly came to a close. Rochester got approval to spend the planning funds for the university center. The trout stream in Savage was addressed to Representative Wolf's satisfaction. The Republican caucus got everything it wanted.

My bonding maneuver had worked to perfection.

CHAPTER 5

{ Legislating and the }
News Media

L egislators will not last long in office unless they stay in
touch with the people who elected them.

There are multiple ways for legislators to communicate
directly with their constituents. These include personal con-
tacts, telephone calls, and written communication. All these
approaches are important. However, direct contact must also
be supplemented by indirect communication via the media.
Legislators need to appreciate journalists as a powerful
resource for transmitting information.

Members of the news media, with the power they possess
to communicate to the public, should be treated almost as
if they hold a gavel. This means lawmakers need to be available, responsive, and respectful. The overriding standard for
journalists is to be impartial, truthful, and objective.

As a legislator, I interacted with members of the media
in several different ways. The *Rochester Post-Bulletin* had a
very curious and capable reporter assigned to the press room
in the capitol. Local radio stations assigned reporters who
called me for voice interviews, and Jane Belau ran interviews
on Rochester television weekly during the session and also at

the end of each session. I was also a frequent guest on Twin Cities Public Television's statewide program, *Almanac,* where current issues were debated.

It is especially important for lawmakers to use the media if they want to get serious or controversial legislation approved. I tried to use the media in this way as a force for persuasion, just as I would use a caucus, lobbyists, the governor's staff, or any other potential source of support. I first had to persuade the reporters that what I wanted them to write about was worthwhile. Persuading the people who are going to cover a bill is as important as persuading the other legislators.

So what are the steps legislators should take to work effectively with the media? First they should identify all reporters who cover the geographic area they represent or who follow their subject areas and major committees. In Minnesota, the two largest newspapers each have several reporters covering the legislature when it is in session. Lawmakers should meet these people, try to establish a good rapport with them personally, and also explain their legislative agenda. The media are good sounding boards for most ideas. Getting any kind of positive response is an excellent indicator of the legislator's ability to persuade.

If a lawmaker provides information to the media early, and thoroughly, reporters will be educated about an issue when it comes time for a hearing. An educated media is friendlier than one still trying to figure out the basics of a proposal and it will do a better job reporting the issues accurately. Legislators must not hold back information, particularly if they know that there is serious opposition to their idea or proposal. Reporters will find out if someone wants to kill a lawmaker's bill anyway, and by providing this information up front, legislators will establish credibility and spark the media's interest.

Still, legislators should wait until they really have something to say before talking with reporters because journalists do not want to be bothered with preliminary material. They want to be brought in when something is already underway because so many bills and ideas are competing for their attention. Sometimes legislators who go to the press too soon get lots of media attention but no lasting effect.

When information is provided early it may need to be labeled as background only, giving the media some framework for proposals that will appear later. It is a green apple—the media can't be allowed to pick it. Reporters will need to be told when the story is ripe. Legislators should notify the media when they have hearings scheduled for their proposals. Reporters should be contacted personally and given access to background materials, as well as the research and handouts legislators will be using.

Once legislators provide information to the media, they must follow up frequently. They must keep connected and touch base whenever something happens. These events might include a bill moving in a committee or a new supporter coming on the scene. My practice was to stop by the capitol press room after floor sessions to visit with my local reporter to see if we had information to exchange. I would let the reporter know if anything was happening with my bills and what I was planning for the next week. I would receive information from him on what was going on in my hometown. It was a cooperative relationship that helped both of us.

By establishing a good relationship with the reporter, the legislator gets an opportunity to present his or her case. Nine times out of ten, the stories the reporter writes will be read by fellow reporters in the state. Those colleagues then have their interest sparked to start asking questions. They may end up doing their own versions of the story. The issue snowballs, and all of a sudden your bill or idea is getting broad exposure.

Some elected officials from rural areas have several small weekly newspapers in their district, but no daily. It is usually easier to get the attention of these papers than that of the major media. Small-town media don't usually have staff assigned to the capitol, so they like to have their elected officials provide them with press releases or interviews. It is important to know how to position yourself with the media. Sometimes you need to direct them to their places, set the stage, and make them do some work. And it doesn't hurt for you to create some mystery and suspense.

CASE: Northwest Airlines and a Sales Tax

In 1990, Rochester leaders wanted to renew the special local sales taxes I had helped persuade the legislature to approve seven years earlier. The 1983 taxes had helped pay the bonds for the flood-control project and civic center. Now, the city wanted the one-percent tax for a new government center, an enlarged library, and a new fire hall that would be large enough to handle equipment for protecting twenty-story buildings.

My Republican colleagues from Rochester, Senator Nancy

Brataas and Representative Gil Gutknecht, were chief authors of the renewed tax legislation. Gutknecht got it passed in the house, but it was blocked in the senate by Doug Johnson, the DFL chairman of the Tax Committee. He did not like local sales taxes. He thought the state should be the source of all public revenue and that local sales taxes created inequities by favoring wealthy communities over poorer ones. So how were we going to get around him?

The answer, surprisingly, had to do with a timely newspaper article and one of the state's largest employers at that time, Northwest Airlines.

In 1991, Northwest was on the ropes financially. The company wanted to borrow $320 million from the Metropolitan Airports Commission, a governmental body that operates the Minneapolis–St. Paul International Airport, and it needed another $50 million to build a repair facility in St. Louis County, in northern Minnesota. Legislators from Duluth and the surrounding area were quite excited about this project. The governor at the time, Arne Carlson, also supported it.[1]

However, the issue had been highly controversial during the 1991 legislative session. Many voters viewed assisting Northwest as a government bailout of a private company and publicly opposed helping.[2]

Legislators are like turtles. They don't want to stick their necks out when they can smell a storm. Sensing trouble with the question of whether to aid Northwest, legislative leaders kicked the issue over to the eighteen-member bipartisan Legislative Commission on Planning and Fiscal Policy (LCPFP). That's where I came in. I had been a member of the commission ever since Senator Jerry Hughes and I had authored the legislation that created it in 1986.[3]

The Minnesota legislature was between sessions and I was away from the capitol, finishing my Master of Public Administration degree at Harvard's Kennedy School of Government, when this issue began to heat up. I had employed an assistant, Tom Keliher, to monitor the commission hearings and keep me informed. I also talked often with Northwest's general counsel and treasurer. I knew how critical the issue was to northern Minnesota—the home, by the way, of Senator Johnson, who was blocking renewal of the Rochester sales levy.

One day, Keliher told me a decision on Northwest was imminent and that I needed to come back to Minnesota. I started getting ready to go. The day before I planned to leave Harvard, I got a call from Bruce Orwall, a reporter for the *St. Paul Pioneer Press*. He said he was taking a poll of commission members on the Northwest issue.[4]

"I'm on the fence," I told him. I had consciously decided to cast myself as an undecided vote, but what I said was still sincere. I did support Northwest Airlines, but I also felt the proposal needed some work.

"I'll put you down as undecided," Orwall said.

The next day the *Pioneer Press* reported that the Northwest assistance package seemed to be up in the air, with three of eighteen commission members undecided and the rest about evenly split for and against the airline.

When I got back to my room after my last class, just before I was about to leave for Minnesota, there was a phone message on the answering machine.

"Dave, this is Doug Johnson," said the message. "I really need to talk to you right away. Give me a call."

When I called him, we exchanged a little small talk. Then he said, "Dave, I read in the *Pioneer Press* that you're on the fence about the Northwest deal." He paused. "Dave, this is awfully important."

"Doug, I still have to look this over," I said. "But don't worry, I'll be back in time for the Monday meeting."

"Come and see me right away when you get here," he said.

When I got back, I went over to Johnson's office. He and the Northwest executives were there and they summarized the proposal for me, but I wasn't ready to commit. I had concerns about the state's authority to issue the loans and said I needed to work up an amendment.

Next I met with fellow commission members Representative Dee Long and Senator Ember Reichgott Junge, both of whom were Democrats. We drafted an amendment that said the state had authority to make the loan transactions, but if Northwest was about to default, the state had to be notified and given a voice. Another part of the amendment said no more than half of the $270 million loan from the airports commission could be used to prepay debt from the leveraged buyout and that the loan for St. Louis County had to be secured by tools, parts, and equipment—a dollar and a half of appraised market value for every dollar of the loan. The amendment also had provisions that pressured Northwest to maintain jobs and flights in the state.

Now I felt comfortable supporting the Northwest package. I presented the amendment to the LCPFP. When it came up by roll call, the vote was eleven for and seven against. The collaborative work I had done with Reichgott Junge and Long had been the key to the deal. Both Johnson and DFL congressman James Oberstar were extremely pleased. Oberstar came up to me with strong praise after the vote, which Senator Johnson noticed.[5]

I never mentioned the Rochester sales tax during any of the discussions about Northwest. Johnson didn't bring it up either, yet the sales-tax renewal remained bottled up in Johnson's committee through the 1991 session.

The following year, my Rochester colleagues, Gutknecht and Brataas, again tried to get the sales tax renewed. Once more it looked like something would get through the house, but Johnson was blocking it as vigorously in 1992 as he had in 1991.

"I think I can help," I told Gutknecht. "But you have to tell me that you really need it because I don't want to play my trump card unless it is absolutely necessary." I told Brataas the same thing.

Shortly afterward, Gutknecht came to me in the house retiring room and told me that Jim Erickson, Rochester's hired lobbyist, had told him it looked bad for the tax renewal. Gutknecht also said Johnson's committee was going to meet the following day.

I went over to the senate floor and found Brataas. "We're not going to get it," she told me. "Dougie's got it bottled up. You'd better do what you can do."

I went to Johnson's office. The door was closed. I knocked and opened it up. Ron Jerichs, Johnson's close friend, was sitting there with him. Johnson invited me in. I remember thinking how unusual it must be for a house minority member to be dropping in on the senate Tax Committee chairman.

"What can I do for you?" he asked.

I told him I understood he was holding up the Rochester sales-tax renewal.

"Yes," he said, "I don't like it. I don't like local sales taxes."

"Doug, you remember when you needed help," I told him. "Now I need help."

"Well, Dave," he said, "you know I've always been strongly opposed to a local sales tax. I'm not going to change my position."

"Doug, you don't have to change your position," I said. "You can remain opposed. All you have to do is pick up your phone and let your majority members know you are freeing them to vote against you, that you won't be mad if they support our sales tax."

He agreed to do this and the senate Tax Committee then approved the sales-tax renewal. The logjam was broken. I had built a bridge that was there when I needed it. And my "undecided" comment reported in the media had helped jump-start the conversation. My work with Johnson on the Northwest Airlines bill meant he would be willing to listen to my ideas and consider my requests. While I could have called Congressman Oberstar for help, it was never necessary.

CHAPTER 6

Lawmakers Get An Idea, Now What?

Ideas for legislation usually come from a few key sources. The administration may have a bill that fits its agenda. Community organizations or groups often have ideas for legislation that they need help getting passed. Other times an issue can come from the public or be in response to an event. It wasn't unusual for me to find ideas for legislation in the newspapers.

In July 1986, I read a story about an underground pipeline that had ruptured, sending gasoline flowing through neighborhood streets in the early morning hours in the St. Paul suburb of Mounds View. Exhaust from the car of a newspaper carrier ignited gasoline vapors, causing a fiery explosion. A woman and her seven-year-old daughter were awakened by the blast and left their home, only to be killed in a subsequent explosion and fire as gasoline from the ruptured pipe continued to flow. More than two hundred people were evacuated.[1]

I was shocked. What was the pipeline problem? Then I read that Governor Rudy Perpich was putting together a task force to examine issues related to the accident. I called his office and asked to be part of it. At that time, I was chairman of the Energy Subcommittee of the house Regulated Industries and Energy Committee, so it made sense for me to participate. The task force investigations disclosed shoddy federal-government pipeline surveillance. This motivated me to try drafting a bill to improve standards for pipeline safety. DFL senator Steve Novak, who represented the Mounds View area, collaborated with me. This, by the way, was in 1986, while I was still in the majority.

In 1987, our roles reversed. He took over the bill and we worked on it together.

The new law created the state Office of Pipeline Safety. As of 2013, through a mix of state and federal funding, the Minnesota office had conducted over fifty-nine hundred inspection hours of pipeline companies throughout the state.[2]

Another way I frequently found ideas for legislation was from my constituents. Ray Schmitz, the Olmsted county attorney, brought a lot of ideas to me. He was concerned, for example, about the responsibility of someone who caused a death through the illegal sale or distribution of certain controlled substances. After talking with him, I drafted a bill that made this second-degree murder. Another bill I wrote for Schmitz made it a felony to solicit sex from a child under the age of sixteen.[3]

My legislative work on behalf of battered women derived from both my personal law practice and my relationship with advocates in Rochester. One of the things that most upset me in my practice was physical abuse by a husband toward his wife. And there'd been few places for women and their children to find safe refuge. Battered women's shelters had developed to provide housing and services, but they were chronically short of funds.

After the end of the 1983 session, I visited Rochester's Women's Shelter, Inc., and met the director, Judy Miller, and also Donna Dunn, the public-education director. At this visit, I learned about another problem battered women were facing. Donna Dunn told me the shelter, though rated by the city for only fourteen persons, was then occupied by twenty-one because women ready to leave had nowhere safe to go. They needed low-cost transitional housing to help them move back into society.

In 1984, Representative Karen Clark came before my State Departments Appropriations Committee with a temporary-housing bill. I offered an amendment that one of three pilot programs would be for "transition housing for persons leaving a shelter for family abuse." The Rochester shelter applied for and was granted a state housing loan that was used to buy a large apartment building for battered women's transition housing.[4]

A few years later, Judy Miller brought to my attention the fact that there was a great need for an international women's shelter. Traditional women's shelters were not able to meet the culturally specific needs of many Asian women and their children, who could not go publicly to a regular shelter. I wrote an amendment, which became part of the omnibus judiciary funding bill, providing support. The resulting shelters, one in Rochester and two in the Twin Cities, were the first of their kind in the country and were used as models for others that followed.[5]

At the time of my retirement, all of the women in both caucuses of the Minnesota House of Representatives posed with me for a photo, to recognize my work on domestic abuse prevention and other women's issues.

One very snowy late December afternoon I invited Governor Carlson to join me on a tour of the new facility in Rochester. Judy showed us around. It got quite late and the governor's staff was anxious to get back on the road. The blizzard was really howling. Just as we were getting ready to leave in our hats and dark coats, a little girl, no more than six, came up to us. She said, "Mr. Governor, Mr. President, my name is America." Years later, when Judy was speaking at my retirement party, she told me that America, now a young woman living and working in Rochester, remembered our visit and was an example of the success the shelter has been.

When someone comes to a policymaker and says, "We

need to change a law," the first question a legislator must ask is, "Does this problem require a legislative action?" It is important to ask the person with the request to put the problem and proposed solution in writing. This written analysis should include who or what the change will benefit, and who it will hurt. When does the issue need to be addressed? How much will it cost? Lawmakers must get and examine this information. Does it look workable? Will it be helpful for everyone, a true public good?

Most ideas have already been tried somewhere else. If the idea is really good, it is likely another state has a similar law. Most legislatures have some type of nonpartisan research staff who can help assemble information about existing law throughout the country. These staff are a very valuable asset for a legislator. They have seen ideas come and go. They can be counted on to give unbiased information and advice. Many researchers have been on the job for many years. They often have long institutional memories and wide experience on the issues. They may have seen the issue in previous legislation and can point out the obstacles ahead of time, saving hours of work while giving the legislator information to use to anticipate trouble spots. They can often tell exactly why a similar idea failed in the past. These people can provide good insights into the strengths and weaknesses of an idea. Because of all these things their work is perceived as reliable and can carry a lot of weight in the legislative debate. Unfortunately, many legislators rely only on their own caucus staff, receiving everything through a partisan filter. In doing so, they miss taking advantage of an important resource that could strengthen their legislation.

FINDING COMMON GROUND

Careful strategy is crucial for moving ideas into laws. If policymakers decide the problem requires legislative action, they should not only draft the proposal but develop a strategy to get it approved. They must analyze the proposed action and likely reaction and try to anticipate conflict. They need to take into account the legislators and lobbyists who are likely to stand with them and against them and determine with whom they will be working and whom they'll need to avoid.

Legislators must learn the subject well enough to make a quick case to the chair or vice chair of each committee to which their proposed legislation is likely to be referred. A majority member from each of those committees should be lined up, if possible, as coauthor.

Many legislators make the mistake of choosing only friends as coauthors. They don't look beyond their immediate circle. This can be very limiting. As a Republican, I would typically choose two or three Democrats and one or two members from my own caucus as coauthors. The majority coauthors would be a chair or other important member of a necessary committee. I preferred to select people with whom I had good relations. And if I didn't have good relations with the necessary committee chairs, I sought coauthors who did. A committee chair as coauthor almost always guarantees the bill a hearing. It also usually acts as a signal of approval to other committee members. Some chairs do not want to be co-opted by signing on as coauthors, however, so they let other members take that role.

The process of choosing an author in the other body works in a similar way. Legislators should not rely just on depart-

{ 84 }

ment staff, the governor's office, or their caucus leaders to find someone appropriate. Instead, they should look at the committee structure and where they expect the bill to move. They should search for an author from among the chairs and committee leaders. As a minority member, I rarely picked a senate minority member as a companion author. Choosing a majority author creates instant bipartisanship and strengthens the bill in both houses. But legislators should certainly choose someone in the other body who represents their district if the bill in question only has local impact.

Unfortunately, lawmakers don't always have complete control over who the companion author will be, especially if the bill is brought to them by a state agency, the governor's office, or a lobbying group. They may end up carrying a bill that is at a dead end in the other house, simply because the instigator chose the wrong author. I once carried a bill for the governor's office on which the senate author was selected for purely political considerations. Because the senator wasn't a member of the right committee, and the chair of the committee to which the bill was sent didn't like him, the bill didn't move at all. We ended up having to switch the author midcourse just to get a hearing, and we lost momentum as a result.

Lawmakers must be careful in choosing a vehicle for their bill. Legislation that gets wrapped into another bill may fail. If legislators saddle up their bill on another member's horse, they may lose control and their idea may get killed because that horse can pull up lame. Often, especially with a simple or uncontroversial issue, moving a bill by itself is better. Ultimately, however, it depends on the bill. Some will succeed only if they are attached to a larger "omnibus" bill, which is a package of germane proposals. Omnibus bills are often created at the end of session when time is tight and there are still so many bills that need action. Sometimes if you're not sure your bill is going to succeed on its own, adding it to an omnibus increases its chances of passage.

Timing and the legislative calendar are important aspects of strategy, as well. Typically the first bills on a committee's agenda get nitpicked by new members trying out their smart questions. Unless there is a strong need to pass something quickly, legislators should consider getting their bills heard later in the session. A successful strategy also means considering rulemaking deadlines. For example, if a bill's sponsors start a bill in the body where it has the most support, there is a better chance of meeting the first legislative deadline for holding a hearing.

The last week before the deadlines for committees to act is one of the best times to have a hearing. If policymakers can get an advance commitment from the chair, they have a lot of time to line up support and allies and to work out any differences with the other body. They shouldn't wait too long, however. People don't realize how compressed the legislative session is. Many things fail because of timing.

Knowing the schedule of when bills will be heard can be helpful. In 1990, Amy Caucutt, the lobbyist for Olmsted County, asked me to carry a bill for an issue that the county board had recommended: joining the offices of county auditor and treasurer. At this time, four larger Minnesota counties already had been approved for reorganization of these two offices in order to provide greater efficiency in land-management functions. I made sure that our bill was timed to be heard in the committee immediately following a similar bill, carried by a freshman Democrat, for Blue Earth County. The opponents of the bill, auditors and treasurers from all over the state who did not want their jobs eliminated, as well as township officers who opposed diminishing the number of elected offices, had brought out a number of legislators who were against the bill. I realized most of these were Republicans. When I noticed that the great majority of Democrats who would be supporting the Blue Earth legislator were not present, I sent my aide, Tom Keliher, to find out what was going on. He found them in a retiring room discussing other legislation, not worried about the freshman's bill because bills of that nature tend to be uncontroversial. But there was conflict within our caucus. The Rochester-area legislators were split on supporting my bill. I knew I was up against a hard fight, and I would need Democratic votes to get my bill passed.[6]

With this in mind, I asked Keliher to tell the Democrats that one of their own was being strongly challenged by mostly rural Republicans who opposed the idea. They said, "We'll be right there," and all came in, so we had a full quorum. Both bills, which were ahead of their time in government efficiency, passed on that day and became law.[7]

Lawmakers should inform, interview, and try to involve the staffs of the governor and executive agencies that will be affected if the bill passes. Gathering support from non-legislative allies is also vital. Legislators can find these allies by thinking about the impact of the bill. What is the natural constituency for the bill? What groups will it benefit? If legislators do their job successfully, they will get outside support from many sources: political parties, the media, special-interest groups, individuals, and professional associations. Legislators should find as many of these friends as possible and not forget to publicize those outsiders' support for the bill. Lawmakers should work with their staffs to line up these allies as witnesses at hearings, both in their own chamber and in the other body.

Communication is another important element of a successful strategy. It is critical for members of the minority, operating from a position without power, to keep majority members informed about their bills. They also should constantly provide information to their allies and the media. Simply stopping coauthors in the hallway for a few minutes and bringing them up to date on the status of the bill, its current opposition, and any changes to language can make all the difference. The allies now have information they need to act intelligently and avoid surprise.

Surprise is no friend of the legislator. Lawmakers sometimes may be tempted to pull a new idea out of their pockets on the floor or in a committee to try to win a tactical victory. If this idea is a surprise, it will probably provoke more opposition than support, and rightfully so. The legislative process depends heavily on investigation and fact gathering, none of which is present when ideas appear to be presented impulsively.

Legislating is hard work, but it is meant to be. It is not uncommon to see legislators spend more time out of their seats than in them. They will be all over the capitol negotiating, attending hearings, planning strategy, and lobbying for their bills in hallways, offices, and cafeterias. They wrestle with good and bad amendments, and interact with the media and the public. The process of creating laws provides citizens with a method for making changes to their lives. Lawmakers listen to those citizens' needs, present their proposals, and fight for the passage of their bills. This allows a level of participatory representation that is critical to our democracy.

CASE: The Living Will

In 1984, while I was still in my first term, minority leader David Jennings asked me to coauthor his bill for living wills. The bill gave legal authority to people to write and sign documents expressing their wishes for or against medical procedures during a terminal illness, before they became unable to express their desires.

My interest in the subject of personal control of end-of-life decisions had begun years ago, with a high-school debate on euthanasia. Years later, while in private law practice in Rochester, I joined Mayo Clinic doctors at a bar-association program on medical and legal problems surrounding organ transplantation and death. This program had rekindled my passion for questions about how individuals can face critical end-of-life decisions effectively and with dignity.

The problem Jennings was addressing was the lack of a legal procedure for a person to express his or her preferences regarding medical care when a terminal illness is involved. Decisions on terminal medical care were causing conflicts among family members and with doctors. People who knew they were dying had no way to effectively communicate or implement their desires. Doctors and families needed written guidance from the patient that might be used when the patient could no longer speak for themselves: the living will.

Over the course of five years, the struggle for passage of the living will required all the legislative strategies I had to offer. It was a lesson in patience and determination.

Republicans won the house majority in 1984, as I've said, and Jennings became the new speaker. He asked me to take the lead on the living will bill in the 1985 session. I always used my background as a trial lawyer to find evidence that would support the bill on which I was working, so I did a great deal of research, including a survey of thirty-five states that had approved similar legislation. I also did a lot of rewriting.

The main opposition I faced in getting the bill enacted was from Minnesota Citizens Concerned for Life, which I mentioned in Chapter 2. They were vigorously against a living will because they thought such laws looked like euthanasia. For them, it wasn't appropriate for individuals to make their own end-of-life decisions. MCCL had become a tremendously powerful force in Minnesota politics using many methods of pressure. They were very involved in selection and endorsement of candidates and had extensive fund-raising resources. They were also fierce in opposing reelection of legislators who had voted against their positions. Legislators knew that if they went against MCCL on anything, the organization might rally against them in the next election and they would be out of a job.

When the 1985 session got underway, Representative Tony Onnen, chairman of the Health Committee, told me he would give my bill a hearing only if Jackie Schwietz, MCCL's chief lobbyist, approved. But she was a powerful and effective force, and she was locked in against my bill, so nothing happened that year.

In 1986, the speaker sent the bill to the Judiciary Committee rather than health so it finally did get a hearing. Even in Judiciary, however, Schwietz's muscle was apparent.

One of the members told me, "Dave, I know it's a good bill, and the right thing to do would be to give you a vote. But I just can't afford to have those people against me."

By "those people," of course, he meant the MCCL.

Other judiciary members told me they would "take a walk," meaning they would plan to leave the Judiciary Committee meeting just before a vote on the living will bill. But they would leave only if I had the tallies to win without them. Otherwise, they would cast a politically safe vote against my bill. I didn't have enough committee support for a hearing, so the legislation failed again.

After the 1986 elections, we Republicans were in the minority again. Having a Democratic majority wasn't the only dynamic to change around the living will. For the first time, some of the senior-citizen groups got vocal in supporting living wills. They put together a new bill and worked with me to include clauses from my prior drafts. The coalition of supporting organizations, led by the senior groups and all of their memberships, also lined up a new senate author for the 1987 session. I remained chief author in the house, even though I was in the minority.

The bill, just like the previous year, was sent to the house Judiciary Committee. The new chairman, Representative Randy Kelly, tried to get the MCCL opposition to collaborate.

Professional mediators were paid from committee funds to look for areas of agreement, but no negotiation took place. Even the use of the term "living will" was opposed.

MCCL paid to have lawyers from its national affiliate, the National Right to Life Committee, fly in to present their own version of the bill. The MCCL version contained a presumption that every now-incompetent person who was terminally ill had wished, when previously competent, to have artificial food and fluids supplied. This presumption would override any written or oral evidence of a person's decision on what medical care was wanted or not wanted during a terminal illness or injury. This effectively gutted the whole idea of a living will, which gave every competent person the right to make these decisions and put them in writing in advance of or during a terminal illness.

This became the central issue over which compromise was impossible. After thirty-five hours of hearings around the state, the committee was unable to agree. No vote was taken in 1987.

In 1988, the coalition and I worked on Judiciary Committee members in both the house and senate. We were gaining legislators who supported the bill. In the house Judiciary Committee, the MCCL's amendment with the presumption language was defeated by one vote. The senate bill was making progress, too. In fact, both the house and senate bills made it to the floors of their respective bodies for the first time.

A huge setback happened when MCCL's amendment was approved on the senate floor. That prompted our coalition senator to pull the bill. The issue was dead for 1988.

By now I was getting frustrated. For five years we had tried and failed. I told the senior-citizen and medical groups that they had to learn how to play political hardball in the same league as MCCL. I told them that in the next elections, they needed to pound on the legislators who were opposed to the living will. I went to my state Republican convention and argued for support of living wills in the party platform, without success. Senior groups worked the issue in the legislative races. Just as I had advised, the seniors targeted the leaders of the opposition. They were effective, and Republican representative Allen Quist lost his reelection bid.[8]

For the 1989 legislative session, the coalition again decided to switch senate authors, this time selecting Senator Ember Reichgott Junge, who was also an attorney from the Minneapolis suburb of New Hope. The seniors hoped that Senator Reichgott Junge would be more effective in lobbying the opposing senators. I was again chief author in the house.

Few changes were made from the previous session's draft. I wrote an amendment making it clear the bill would not apply to incompetent patients who, when they were mentally competent, had not made a written declaration of their health-care wishes. The amendment also required a physician to find the patient to be in a terminal condition for the document to be effective. The new provisions responded to concerns of some members in both houses.

In 1989, I did something different to try strengthening my hand. I decided to try lining up a majority of the house, sixty-eight members, as coauthors. Since house rules allowed only five members to sign on a bill as coauthors, I drafted fourteen identical bills and asked fourteen members to sign as chief authors and to get four more coauthors signed onto each bill. I was building my own coalition. I spent an average of an hour each with about one hundred members, going over the bill and discussing its political ramifications. I got signatures of only sixty-six members, but this sent a strong message to the leadership of both caucuses that this year the bill had strong bipartisan support.[9]

Despite the strong showing, Randy Kelly declared my bill would not get a hearing until the full senate approved its version. He was getting tired of spending committee time and expense on a bill that never seemed to go anywhere. Now it became critical to get senate support from some who had voted against the living will the previous year. Reichgott Junge worked on the senators. The bill went to the senate Judiciary Committee, where it was amended and sent to the floor. The full senate then gave its approval, with only minor amendments. The difference this year was the work done by Senator Reichgott Junge.

Next it was the house's turn.

From the beginning of the 1989 session, one of my most important tasks was to gain support from the Minnesota Catholic Conference, which is the public-policy voice of the Catholic Church in the state. I figured that getting the group's backing would help garner support from legislators who had strong Catholic constituencies. I had attempted this approach in previous years as well. In 1985, I had woven some wording into the bill from the pope's "Declaration on Euthanasia." In hearings, I had used a professor of Christian ethics from a Catholic-oriented private college as a witness.

This year when I went to a dinner for legislators that was

put on by the Catholic Health Association of Minnesota, I told their chief lobbyist, former senator Joe O'Neill, "I really need your help."

"We really want your bill," O'Neill told me, and agreed to assist. "I'll bring some folks to your office and see if we can get it done."

Those folks were the ethicist from the archbishop's office and Monsignor James Habiger, executive director of the Minnesota Catholic Conference. He was a friend of mine from when he had served as house chaplain. I had admired his prayers to open sessions and frequently asked for copies for my files.

In my research for this bill, I received copies of a pamphlet on medical decisions from the Catholic Health Association in St. Louis, Missouri. I showed them and my bill to the men. "Dave," Monsignor Habiger said, "there is nothing in your bill that is contrary to Catholic doctrine. I wish I could say so publicly, but we are so closely connected with MCCL on the abortion issue that we really can't go against them publicly. However, if you have some committee members who would like to know our position, tell them to call me, and I'll tell them what I just told you."

I was eager to take him up on the offer. I suggested to some house Judiciary Committee members that they speak with Monsignor Habiger. This was critical because the understanding that nothing in the legislation violated Catholic teachings gave some committee members enough comfort to vote for the bill against the wishes of MCCL. Two members who had opposed the living will agreed to switch their position.

The Judiciary Committee held a ten-hour hearing on the bill. At the end of it, the panel voted to defeat MCCL's presumption amendment 13–12. The overall bill was then approved by that same margin of one vote. Jackie Schwietz, the MCCL lobbyist, was furious. In a sign of her continuing influence, the two members who had surprised her were later defeated for reelection.

Now the countdown was on for house floor action. I personally reached out to about eighty members. The opposition brought in national association officers from Washington. Senior groups brought hundreds to the capitol for a rally in support. We passed out big buttons that said, "Let Me Decide." Media coverage was heavy.

Both sides met with Governor Rudy Perpich, who had been strongly pro-life on abortion questions. He listened, and indicated he would sign the bill if it passed, although he would not publicly press for it.

The house floor fight arrived on schedule. Some minor amendments, such as adding extra warnings about artificial feedings, were added. All the lobbying we had done against the MCCL presumption amendment paid off. The amendment that had killed the bill in the senate the previous year went down in the house, with sixty-three in favor and seventy against. The final vote on the bill was 102–31, but it was anticlimactic after defeating the MCCL amendment.

The senate concurred with the house version and Perpich held a huge signing ceremony for the first major bill to be enacted in the 1989 session. What an exciting moment!

After six years of political battle, the new legislation took effect. Four million citizens in Minnesota, including one

CHAPTER 7

The Tricky Dance

All my life, I've enjoyed dancing. When I learned to dance, it was with a partner, where one person leads, or controls the other, in this traditional style of dancing. Whether the dance is a waltz, a foxtrot, or a tango, the leader chooses the steps and the direction or path the couple takes across the dance floor. The partner can suggest moves or give signals but is expected to follow the leader.

Modern dance is different. Sometimes people dance by themselves, sometimes with a partner. Often they dance to the same music in entirely different and independent ways. One person may sometimes be more in control than the other, but not always.

In most legislatures, the majority leads in a traditional-style dance. The minority is the partner with limited motion. If the majority dips, the minority must follow. But the legislative style I prefer could be called the "tricky dance." This type of dancing involves careful political maneuvering. You have to move your feet quickly without stepping on anyone's toes. Though the dance begins in a traditional manner, with the majority in control, at some point the minority partner makes a new move and becomes more independent. The majority partner responds and picks up the move. This approach fits more with the modern style of dancing in which both partners follow the music, but each is able to make independent moves.

Many of the principles of successful dancing apply in the legislative context. Legislators must be attractive to their partners. They have to be positive and trustworthy. They must share the same goals (for the legislation they are working on) and be loyal to each other (until the bill is passed). But the parallels don't end with being a pleasant, accommodating, and unthreatening partner. Each legislator must use careful footwork with his or her partner to reach the common goal.

I was at a hearing for the budget of the Legislative-Citizen Commission on Minnesota Resources. The commission's members were some of the most powerful legislators from both caucuses and chambers. Meeting only when the rest of the legislature was out of session, they focused on long-term needs as opposed to conference bills and funds. Collaboration was the norm and the confrontation associated with sessions and partisanship was rare.

Being at the hearing gave me the idea that this type of collaborative approach should be used for our state-budget process. Our Appropriations and Finance Committees were having chronic problems balancing the budget. We didn't do any long-term fiscal planning, even for major challenges such as funding public schools and health care. I decided to try creating a fiscal-policy commission modeled after the one for natural resources.[1]

I shopped the concept to some senior majority members. The president of the senate, Jerry Hughes, agreed to be that body's chief author. I asked DFL representatives Gordy Voss and Wayne Simoneau if they would help put it together and support it in the house. They did and signed on as coauthors, with me as chief author.

In 1987, the Legislative Commission on Planning and Fiscal Policy became a reality. The creation of this fiscal-planning commission was an example of the minority dancing partner becoming liberated and being innovative.[2]

Still, minority legislators must watch out that they don't cooperate so thoroughly with the majority that they alienate their own caucus. The cliché is "When the evening is over, you go home with the one who brung ya." Legislators must work with their own caucus on critical issues such as taxes, budgets, and major financing bills. These issues usually define the philosophical and partisan divisions between the caucuses.

Before minority members work with members of the other party, they should make their caucus leadership understand that the joint effort is limited to a specific issue. If they don't communicate effectively ahead of time, their own caucus members might misunderstand and block the dancer's bipartisan efforts.

Legislators do need to be alert and light on their feet. The group they work with on one bill may be the group they oppose on another. They can have partners who are close friends, or they can create alliances that are distant and fragile. Some partnerships can be ad hoc, formed just for the passage of a specific bill. Lawmakers may unite with these partners again, but generally they are trying to tailor their alliances for a specific legislative situation.

Minority legislators may also decide to surrender their

idea to the majority. If I concluded that a proposal of mine needed a majority house author in order to pass in the senate, I would take it to a committee chair so he or she could get the credit. I'd offer to help as a coauthor. This is also an important bridge-building tool, because the chairs would know I was not trying to embarrass them. They would trust me more in the future as a result.

One caution about the tricky dance: sometimes the majority partners like your steps so much, they take over and claim responsibility for the new dance craze—even when you don't want them to and haven't made the offer. As Harry Truman once said, "It is amazing what you can accomplish if you do not care who gets the credit." A minority member must be prepared for this eventuality, especially if his or her idea is politically attractive. The most important part of the bill is the final result, not the name of the individual who sponsored it.

CASE: Moving the Historical Society

An example of a time when I had to carefully maneuver among many different principal players involved the new historical society building. In 1984, when I was a member of the state departments division of the House Appropriations Committee, we were trying to figure out where to situate a new building for the judiciary. Two years earlier, with the passage of a constitutional amendment, Minnesota had created an appellate court. Since then the judiciary had been leasing temporary space for this new court in downtown St. Paul. Now we wanted to combine offices for the supreme

court with those for the new appellate court and related services into one building.

The committee hired a Minneapolis architect, Leonard
Parker, to report on the ten best sites for the new building.
Parker told the committee the best option would be to use
some state-owned land near the capitol, on which the Minnesota Historical Society occupied a building. He said, however, that the site was not available.

"Why not?" I asked him.

He said Russ Fridley, the historical society director, had
reached an agreement with Minnesota Supreme Court chief
justice Doug Amdahl that the property would continue to
serve the society's needs. The society had outgrown its space
but wanted to stay at its existing location with a renovation
and expansion. The judiciary would have to look elsewhere.

"Madam Chair," I said to the committee chair, Representative Phyllis Kahn. "Whose decision is it to select the site
for a judicial building? Is it to be made by the judiciary, the
historical society, or the legislature?" Committee members
and Parker chuckled, but they got my point.

My exchange with Parker at the committee got me thinking. What really would be the best location for this new judicial building, regardless of any supposed agreements that had
been made? A few days later, as I traveled to work from my
apartment in downtown St. Paul, I looked at our magnificent capitol. The 1905 building, which had brought national
fame to its architect, Cass Gilbert, is perhaps the finest state
capitol in the country. As the pinnacle of our capitol com-
pound and the symbol of our democracy, it was thrilling for
me to view.

The capitol building is flanked on both sides by grey stone structures of monumental and classical architecture. The State Office Building, on the left, was my destination that morning. To the right was the historical society building, which reminded me of the US Supreme Court building in Washington, DC, also designed by Gilbert. The facade of this building had Greek corniced columns and a stone staircase, and its red-tile pitched roof matched that of the State Office Building.

An early version of the capitol-complex design had intended the state supreme court to occupy the site that became the offices for the historical society. The planned use was changed some years later when the legislature decided to keep the supreme court offices in the capitol building itself. As a result of this decision, the site was turned over to the historical society in 1913 and funds were appropriated for construction of the current building.[3]

A powerful thought struck me. We legislators would have a once-in-a-lifetime opportunity to have these three buildings represent and function as the three independent branches of our state government: the legislative, executive, and judicial. If we put the judiciary somewhere else, the decision would hold for at least a hundred years and waste this opportunity.

I was personally sold on my idea, but wondered how to pitch it to other legislators. Ultimately the choice for this project would be made by the Appropriations Committee, so I decided to seek help from the committee's vice chairman, David Battaglia of Two Harbors. He liked my idea and agreed to help.

Battaglia's motivation was strengthened when we learned that the historical society planned to move Minnesota's first locomotive, the William Crooks, from its temporary home at the Lake Superior Railroad Museum in Duluth. The Minnesota Historical Society had loaned the locomotive to the museum and now planned to bring it back to St. Paul, where it could live in the society's newly enlarged building. The citizens of Two Harbors, however, wanted to keep the locomotive in the Duluth area.

When we went to see Chief Justice Amdahl, he told us the judiciary no longer had any interest in the historical society building and instead favored a site north of the capitol, on top of a nearby hill. He also affirmed what Parker had told us. He had agreed he wouldn't try to displace the historical society from its current location.

Battaglia and I then went to see Fridley, the historical society director. I told him of our idea. He asked me what future I had in mind for his office, where we were sitting for our meeting. I looked out the window and said, "This would be just right for the chief justice." He seemed amused but not persuaded.

Next we went to see Governor Rudy Perpich and I told him about our plan. He was quite positive. I heard that after our meeting, some in the judiciary lobbied Perpich to try to change his mind. Supreme court justice Lawrence Yetka and appellate court chief judge Peter Popovich had invited Perpich to dinner a few times to persuade him to oppose my plan. So after these dinners, Battaglia and I had to go back to Perpich to make our case again. I told Perpich, "Governor, you really don't want the judiciary sitting up on that hilltop looking down on governors for the next hundred years, do you?" He thought about it and laughed.

Fridley didn't like my idea any more than the judiciary did. He orchestrated a statewide counterattack by his large historical society membership. The society's effort included editorials opposing my idea in both Twin Cities newspapers. Their effort got so intense that Battaglia and I had to lobby every Appropriations Committee member personally to try to get their support.

Finally the full Appropriations Committee adopted our plan. Then my house colleagues, led by Battaglia, persuaded senators in the 1984 conference committee. It was tense but exciting.

After the 1984 elections, Republicans took over the house. New house speaker David Jennings appointed me as our body's member on the Capitol Area Architecture and Planning Board, which had previously opposed our plan vigorously.

I was also appointed to an architect's jury, which included Yetka and Popovich as well. An important clause we had put into the legislation required any plan for the new court facilities to incorporate the old structure. The jurors met in St. Paul for several days and looked at proposed plans from nationally regarded architects. The submissions were anonymous and color coded, and all but one of the jurors voted for the design coded purple. Imagine our surprise when we learned that the winning design had been submitted by Leonard Parker, the architect from Minneapolis who had started the whole idea. What poetic justice![4]

An editorial cartoon by Jerry Fearing of the *St. Paul Dispatch* showed the intense interest in the plan to move the Minnesota Historical Society.

I continued the mission when I was on the bonding-bill conference committees. The conference committee helped to fund first the new Minnesota History Center in 1987, and then in 1992 the new Judicial Center. The net result was a magnificent addition to our capitol complex, one which preserves the old historical society building's classical exterior. Our vision allows the capitol complex to truly represent the three branches of our government with classical buildings beautiful in both design and function.[5]

CHAPTER 8

{ The Legislator's Toolbox }

A s a member of the minority for all but six years of my twenty-year legislative career, I used many tools, tactics, and methods to get support from those who had the power to help my bills. This chapter reveals some of those approaches. If used correctly, they can help many legislators accomplish their policy goals.

1. Legislators Must Do Their Homework

Constituent services should be a top priority for all legislators. This means answering phone messages, e-mails, and letters. It also means reading local newspapers to learn about problems that could use a legislative solution. Legislators should attend local meetings on political subjects and be available to meet with individuals and groups. An elected representative must be a listener to those he represents as well as an advocate for needed changes in existing laws.

Perhaps the most important work a legislator can do in order to support a bill is to look for outside evidence to persuade colleagues. This means meeting with research staff and identifying where the idea has been tried before and what happened to it.

Another part of a legislator's homework is to build group support on almost every bill. Legislating is group work and lawmakers need as many members of coalitions as possible to get fingerprints on their bills. They should consult with coalition representatives, let them help with bill wording, and have them attend hearings. This broadens the number of people who feel ownership of a solution. A major hazard to good policymaking is when authors believe they know so much about a subject that they think they can go it alone.

2. Lawmakers Must Be Lobbyists

Legislation is only accomplished by lobbying, which means persuading others of the need for change and of the desirability of the proposed solution. Chief authors of bills need to lobby their colleagues. The biggest mistake many legislators make is to assume that if they have a good idea, it will sell itself. They believe that if there is no obvious opposition, their ideas will move forward. I have seen the most powerful committee chairs propose significant bills and lose them because they didn't attempt to persuade anyone.

Unfortunately many legislators also rely more on authority than persuasion. They put too much trust in the symbolism and apparent authority of office, whether it is that of the governor or a majority or minority leader. They don't spend enough time thinking about the policy implications of their proposals and don't make enough of an effort to promote the merits of their ideas to colleagues.

Legislators must ask themselves who is needed to support

the idea or bill. They should lobby the majority members of the first committees that will hear their proposed legislation. I can't stress enough how important this is.

Potential allies need to know the reasons legislators are carrying a bill. Allies also need to know what the legislators understand about the subject, what changes they will accept, and any potential unintended consequences. Lawmakers must reach out to these potential allies quickly, before someone else gets those same people to oppose the idea.

3. Lawmakers Need to Use Personal Touches

Legislators should contact potential allies personally, whether the allies are inside or outside the legislature. People want to hear directly from policymakers. It is not the same if legislators say, "The staff will contact you." A person-to-person approach is far more effective.

As soon as lawmakers get an idea for legislation, they must prepare to make the sale. They should put together a one-page summary with a statement of the problem and the proposed solution, then ask potential coauthors for ten minutes to sit down together while these others read the summary. Legislators should be reliable and responsive. They should answer phone calls, talk with staff, and let people know when hearings are scheduled. Visiting the other body is important for finding out how companion bills are moving and determining what work remains to be done. Some days, I spent considerable time listening to the discussion of my companion bills on the floor of the senate.

Humor is often a good tool for persuasion and lawmakers should look for opportunities to use it. On many occasions, humor helped me defuse tension and put people at ease.

4. Persistence is Critical

Legislators should earn a reputation for integrity, consistency, and perseverance. When a proposal hits resistance, more work is needed to respond to the opposition. Legislators should do more research, perhaps using research staff to look for a solution to a similar problem in another state. If a bill gets stalled in one legislative session, lawmakers should try it again in the next session, perhaps with changed authors. They should not give up.

5. Vote Counting is Crucial

Whenever a bill or amendment comes up for a vote, authors must know they have lined up the votes necessary to win. They should use their allies from either caucus and check the numbers. If they come up short, they will need to postpone the vote, asking leaders to lay it on the table while the legislators work the members again.

6. Legislators Must Remember Timing

Lawmakers should be informed about the potential timing for hearings in each committee to which their bill may be sent. They also need to watch their companion bill in the other body and its timing, which will have an effect on the proposal in their own body. Legislators must monitor deadlines, know when witnesses who will testify in favor of their bill at a hearing will be available, and do all they can to avoid surprises.

Lawmakers need to look for time to get genuine deliberation for their bills. Deliberation is a necessity for group decision-making and is the antithesis of executive style. Everyone seeks quick decisions on clear choices, but postponement and delay are often needed to deal with complexities in the legislative process.

7. Germaneness Is Important

Lawmakers must remember the principle of germaneness. For a proposed amendment to a bill to be germane, it must be related to the basic subject of the legislation. Legislators must be alert to the possibility of turning a stalled proposal into an amendment to a bill on a similar subject that is coming onto the floor.

8. Legislators Must Watch Bill Wordings

Lawmakers must learn to carefully word their bills. They need to pay close attention to what others may understand about the meanings of the words in bills, and watch out for unintended consequences.

A great deal of legislative debate is over words, not positions or money or actions. When a couple of legislators move into the hallway to work over an issue, it may appear they are cutting a deal. More likely, they are struggling over language, trying to come up with a different word or phrase.

In 1995, I worked on a bill regarding punitive damages against medical-device manufacturers. I got worried when I saw anti-abortion lobbyists monitoring the hearing. I realized the wording of a section that limited damages in claims against the device makers also protected manufacturers of RU-486, the morning-after pill. The lobbyists wanted to preserve the right to sue these manufacturers. This was such a subtle issue that many people had no idea why the lobbyists were so agitated and concerned. They couldn't see the potential meaning and impact of the words. I realized this ominous possibility and watched. It passed without amendment.

9. Lawmakers Should Consider Diversionary Tactics

Sometimes lawmakers can help themselves by proposing counterlegislation to prevent action by an opposing side. The strategy can be controversial and is best saved for special cases, but it can also be effective.

In 1995, I was apprehensive about a potential change in law that would make it more difficult for municipalities to annex townships. Small- and medium-sized cities like the one I represented, Rochester, were growing in population, but they were often blocked by surrounding townships when the cities were trying to expand their boundaries. The townships were defensive, saying, "We run this territory and the people who live here look to us for leadership. We oppose your annexation." My own view was that the township governments were too small, too restrictive, and too out of date in dealing with urban and suburban problems.

To prevent the law, I decided to draw the fire of a very

powerful lobby, the Minnesota Association of Townships, which represented more than eighteen hundred townships in our state. I authored a bill to abolish townships altogether.

My strategy worked. I received many letters, phone calls, and negative editorials in weekly newspapers around the state. This was exactly what I wanted. I was doing something I believed in, but it also had a tactical benefit, similar to a battlefield diversion. I never got a hearing on my bill, but I did get a lot of noise and worry.

Most importantly, throughout the entire session, no legislation was passed that made it more difficult for cities to annex townships. The townships were too preoccupied fighting my diversionary tactic.

CASE: Changing the Speed Limit

Over the course of many years, my work to change the speed limit used almost all of the tools in my toolbox.

In 1985, I decided that Minnesota's 55-mph speed limit needed to be raised. The limit had been in place since 1974, when DFL governor Wendell Anderson established it to comply with a federal mandate related to the worldwide oil embargo. A dozen years later, the reason for the federal executive order no longer existed. The cost of imported oil was not a threat to energy security.

Plus, an overwhelming majority of Minnesota drivers were driving faster than the limit. Even though they were disobeying the law, I felt they were driving safely, most of the time at the speed of the prevailing traffic. As a lawyer, I felt the legislature's statutes should both fit with the commonly accepted practices of the public and be respected by everyone. There was no point to having a law on the books that was so widely ignored.

I had some previous exposure to road designs and safe traveling speeds because I had done legal work for a property owner in 1958 when the two-lane US Highway 52 was widened to four lanes. Now I went to the Minnesota Department of Transportation's Rochester office to look at data. My research supported my position that a higher speed limit wouldn't harm safety. I drafted a simple bill to make 65 mph the limit for four-lane highways.

My bill got a hearing in the Transportation Committee during the session. A state Department of Transportation official said passage of the bill would provoke the federal government to cancel several million dollars of highway grants. I got only one vote in support, and the issue died for the 1985–86 session.

I was driven to persist. For Minnesotans who did obey the law, collectively driving millions of miles at a speed slower than necessary was an enormous waste of valuable time. In the 1987–88 session, I tried the bill again. It was passed by the Transportation Committee and referred to the Appropriations Committee where it died, even though the Congress was now allowing higher speed limits.[1]

I continued. In 1989, I was again blown away by the Transportation Department and the Minnesota State Patrol, which claimed that higher speeds would increase deaths. They presented no evidence for this claim.

During the 1991–92 session, I got a hearing on the same

old bill but with a new number. I offered the committee the findings of studies by the National Highway Traffic Safety Administration. The documents showed highway safety was greatest when people drove their vehicles within 15 mph of the speed of the prevailing traffic. It also showed that 70 percent of fatalities occurred at speeds under 40 mph. Yet I never could get my bill out of the committee for a floor vote.[2]

Then, in 1996, after ten years of efforts off and on, I was on the house floor when a transportation funding bill was about to come up for a debate and vote. This legislation dedicated funds for roads, bridges, transit, and pedestrian safety. It was a possible horse to saddle with a speed-limit amendment. I sent for my file and had the revisor staff draft an amendment: 65 mph for four-lane highways. I quickly got several colleagues from both caucuses to sign on and had it printed and distributed. Though I had not developed a coalition of supporters specifically for this amendment, my colleagues knew well my position.

The arguments I had been making for years in committee were exciting and fun to make to the full house. Very little opposition surfaced. The amendment passed.

I quickly took a copy of the amendment over to DFL senator Leo Foley, who had gone through law school after retiring from the highway patrol. He was eager to help and was able to put my amendment into Senator Keith Langseth's bill. The amended bill passed in the senate, too.

I was feeling quite elated over this success. Then I got a phone call from John Conner, an aide to Governor Arne Carlson. He said, "Dave, I'm sorry to tell you, but Governor

Carlson is expecting to veto the speed-limit increase. He thinks it will be a safety issue, as the state patrol has told him."

"John," I said, "can you get me some time with the governor?"

"Okay, if I can I'll call you." He could and he did, and I went to see the governor.

"Dave, I know you worked hard on this," Governor Carlson told me. "But the state patrol has persuaded me that a speed-limit increase is not a good idea from the safety point of view because the extra speed will mean more accidents, injuries, and deaths."

"Governor," I said, "I brought my file so I could show you some research."

First, I showed him the National Highway Traffic Safety Administration's report. Carlson looked it over.

Then I said, "Here, I want to show you a copy I made from the plans of the Transportation Department for Highway 52 when it was made into a four-lane in the 1950s." I pointed to one item. "Governor, see what is stamped on the plans— 'Design Speed: 70 mph.' There was no seat-belt requirement back then, no air bags, no crash-protecting glass, yet 70 mph was the design speed. I only want 65."[3]

"Okay, Dave," Carlson said. "I'll sign it."

After the new speed limit was enacted into law, there were a few letters to the editor in local newspapers criticizing the change. But I also received a lot of personal thanks from people for this legislative work.

Later, I obtained a copy of the letter a state Department of Transportation district engineer wrote to a Zumbrota woman. This woman had claimed the higher speed limit led to a fatal accident on Highway 52. The engineer told her there had been several studies made of speed and accidents, both before and after the change. He said there was evidence from these studies that Highway 52 was a safer road with the higher speed limit than it had been with a 55-mph standard. In fact the study stated that both compliance decreased and accidents tended to increase when speed limits were lowered. Conversely, when compliance improved after speed limits were raised, accidents tended to decrease.[4]

In the more than two decades since Minnesota adopted these higher speed limits, the state has never looked back. I believe people have benefited from greater efficiency and productivity as a result of the higher speeds. And just as that engineer who wrote the Zumbrota woman found, safety has never suffered.

CASE: The Minority Amendment that Moved a Majority's Mountain

In the second year of each biennium, the legislature appropriates funds to pay for shortfalls from the previous year's appropriations. The perfect example of the tool of germaneness came when the house took up the 1999 deficiency bill.

In 1998, house Republicans won a majority for the first time since the 1984 elections. The new speaker was Steve Sviggum. He appointed me chairman of the Ways and Means Committee, which controls most of the tax and many of the spending decisions in the state. It was a powerful position, and I was glad to get it, although its time demands sharply reduced my ability to work my own bills. In making this appointment, Sviggum acknowledged my sixteen years as a loyal caucus member of Appropriations. As soon as my appointment was made public, the lobbyist for Minnesota Citizens Concerned for Life went to Speaker Sviggum's office to complain. I happened to be present. He told her, "I make these appointments."

Soon after I began my new role in February 1999, the committee's chief fiscal analyst, Bill Marx, brought me a list of spending items for the appropriation package known as the deficiency bill. The bill gets its name because the state would be deficient in its ability to meet these obligations without more action by the legislature.

Marx's list showed more money was needed to support a range of activities, including state services for the blind, the Minnesota Zoo, and legal costs for the defense of lawsuits against schools by the NAACP. The state also needed more money to produce license plates thanks to unexpected demand. State troopers were on the list because they had run up unexpected costs guarding the newly elected governor, Jesse Ventura, at his private home in Maple Grove.

Altogether, the deficiency bill items added up to $17 million. That was very little money by state standards. It amounted to less than one-tenth of one percent of the total two-year budget, which was nearly $33 billion. The low cost, combined with an understanding that the state must pay its bills, typically would make the deficiency proposal uncontroversial. This year was different. The bill became a major test of the new Republican majority's ability to get things done.[5]

I didn't see the conflict coming. The bill appeared routine

while it was being put together in my committee. I authored
it and pushed back on a few items. I didn't like that the zoo
would be getting an additional $1 million. I had struggled for
years with issues of the zoo's management. I felt they didn't
run a tight ship and too often used the state as a resource for
funds when they spent in excess of their budget.

The zoo needed the $1 million mostly because it didn't
get the large increase in attendance it had projected for a
major new exhibit called Discovery Bay. I thought $600,000
would be all right, but not $1 million. I wanted to send zoo
leaders a message and force them to come up with a plan to
either raise the money themselves or cut costs going forward.

I also had concerns about money for attorneys' fees in
the NAACP lawsuits. The Minneapolis and St. Paul school
districts had been sued for allegedly discriminating in the
way they allocated money for pupils. The state attorney general wanted $4.2 million for the costs of defending the two
districts. I thought $3.5 million was more reasonable, but for
the time being I kept the proposal at $4.2 million.

The deficiency bill was passed out of the Ways and Means
Committee at the end of March 1999. The proposal remained
off the radar for most legislators until it came to the house
floor. Then people started questioning the money for Ventura's
security and the zoo. Many of the freshman Republicans, who
had been elected on pledges to cut the budget, looked at the
deficiency bill and said, "Well, this is spending, and we are
supposed to vote against new spending."

When the house clerk called the roll for passage of the bill
on the floor, there were a lot of green "yes" votes from both
caucuses on the board. But then several Republicans started

to put up red "no" votes. When the Democrats saw this, they began to switch from green to red. I couldn't believe it. "Holy smoke!" I said to myself. "This thing is going down!"

I immediately changed my "yes" vote to "no." I had to be on the prevailing side so I would be eligible later to call up the bill for reconsideration. Under house rules, only a legislator who votes with the majority can make a motion to reconsider a bill that has failed. The bill went down on a 74–49 vote.[6]

Our new Republican leadership had made a big tactical mistake. They hadn't counted votes, figuring wrongly that "We'll let our freshman fiscal conservatives vote 'no,' and most of the Democrats will vote 'yes' along with us because it's a routine bill."

Tom Pugh, the house minority leader, later told me that his DFL caucus members didn't think they should have to carry the bulk of the votes since Republicans had criticized them about increased state spending in the previous session.

Now that the deficiency bill had failed, what would I do? I had to try again. I decided I needed to make some changes to win more freshman Republican support. I put in new language saying the zoo had to consider privatizing in order to become self-sufficient. I also reduced the money for defense of the NAACP suits, as I had contemplated earlier, to $3.5 million from $4.2 million.

On April 13, 1999, I brought up the revised deficiency bill on the house floor. This time, our leadership had lined up the Republican votes, and I knew we had enough support to pass it.

Then the strangest thing happened. Pugh, the minority

leader, stood up and proposed to amend the deficiency bill with a massive income-tax cut for all three earnings brackets.[7]

Once again, I was shocked. All through the legislative session, we had struggled to put together a tax bill using more than $1 billion of the excess revenue state-budget forecasters expected by June 30, 1999. The income brackets were currently set at 6 percent, 8 percent, and 8.5 percent, and we Republicans had proposed a half-percent cut in each. Our proposal hadn't been getting anywhere. Governor Ventura had advocated only a quarter-percent cut in the lowest bracket. Democrats also supported a cut only in the lowest bracket.

Now, well into the 1999 session, Pugh seemed to have suddenly adopted the Republican position. He wanted to propose tax cuts in all three brackets and do it in, of all places, the deficiency bill.

Did Pugh have a sudden conversion and become an anti-tax legislator? No. This was strategy. This is what Pugh foresaw: Republicans would decide that the tax proposal was destined for failure in the DFL-controlled senate and therefore would kill the tax provision to ensure safe passage for the deficiency bill. More specifically, he and the house Democrats expected that Speaker Sviggum would find Pugh's tax cut not germane to the deficiency bill and rule it out of order. The Democrats would then ask for a roll-call vote to try to overrule Sviggum's ruling. The Republican majority would vote to uphold Sviggum. Democrats would then be able, in the next election, to point out the vote as an example of the Republicans being two-faced on tax cuts.

But that isn't what happened. None of those Democratic expectations came to be. Sviggum caught the hand grenade the Democrats had thrown at the Republican majority and threw it right back. He ruled Pugh's tax-cut amendment *was* germane to the deficiency bill. Democrats then had no choice but to vote for the amendment they had proposed. The tax cut was approved, 129–1.

I stood up on the house floor and said, "I'm pleased to be the author of the now-largest income-tax cut in the history of the state."

Republican Tim Pawlenty, who was then house majority leader, told me later that the vote on the deficiency bill with the tax cut had changed the dynamic of the session.

"It became a rallying point," Pawlenty said. "The golden ring had now been put within reach. The caucus had finally seen an action that was really meaningful. It was big and dramatic, and it really got people excited. Internally, it helped us a great deal with morale, and it helped us a great deal with team building."

Pugh's amendment had provided the single stroke that united our caucus. For the rest of the session, Republican leaders would say, "We've got to hold onto what was passed on April 13." We went from being a caucus that was broken apart to one that was in control.

The house-approved deficiency bill now went to the senate. The senate didn't know what to do with the bill. So it passed its own deficiency bill, containing no tax cut, and sent it back to the house.

Once the deficiency proposal was back in our chamber, we amended the senate's bill with proposals we Republicans favored, but we didn't add the Pugh tax cut.

A house-senate conference committee was appointed to

reconcile differences between the two bills. Those differences weren't difficult to overcome. For instance, we wound up compromising on the Minnesota Zoo by giving it $800,000. The house's position had been $600,000 and the senate's was $1 million.

Finally, in May, a deficiency bill was passed by both bodies and signed by Ventura.

Also during the 1999 session, the legislature approved a tax bill containing the type of reduction envisioned in the April 13 vote. Taxes were cut by $1.4 billion, the largest amount in state history. All three tax brackets were reduced, to 5.5 percent, 7.25 percent, and 8 percent. The marriage tax penalty was cut, and a $1.3 billion sales-tax rebate was enacted at $600 per taxpayer.[8]

The April 13 vote on the deficiency bill set the stage for the tax cut and became the defining moment of the session. The most important thing we Republicans wanted that year was a substantial tax cut, and the Democrats' amendment to the deficiency bill showed us how to achieve that goal.

CASE: Legislative Failures

Quite a few good ideas that I tried were failures. These taught me many lessons. For example, a failure to properly estimate my opposition sunk a bill to require helmets for motorcyclists. At the first hearing on my proposal, a crowd of black-jacketed motorcycle riders intimidated the Transportation Committee. This was a surprise to me. Also, I had not lobbied committee members or lined up enough votes; I had been that sure of the bill's merits and timeliness.[9]

I remember another failure regarding surrogate parenting. I sympathized with couples who could not conceive children, and I tried to draft a bill that would help them. I used a California law as a model and incorporated my knowledge of Minnesota contract law. But I did not get a large constituency to support the bill: I scheduled a public meeting in downtown St. Paul to discuss the issue, and only a few people came. I received just a few calls on the issue, from potential parents who were inquiring about becoming surrogates. And I encountered tremendous opposition from anti-abortion forces and GOP feminists, who looked at the bill as baby selling. I lost the bill because I incorrectly expected the idea to appeal to a relatively large percentage of infertile couples. This was an example of a failure to have strong constituent support and a failure to get media attention. I also fell short because I tried to do it alone. I had not built a coalition.

The durable power of attorney legislation discussed previously is another example of a time I acted alone with the same unsuccessful result. I was overconfident, assuming that my living will supporters, who had helped me extensively with that bill, would trust me. I didn't realize that I needed to build support for this new idea even with the same constituency. I really didn't learn my lesson until I lost.

Another legislative failure occurred during my first term, in 1983–84. A DFL majority freshman house member, Pat Beard, asked me to coauthor a bill mandating that any state or local government's required purchases could be made only from available Minnesota producers. The bill was popular. It sounded like a good idea, passed in both houses, and was signed into law by Governor Rudy Perpich, taking effect on

August 1, 1983. But the law turned out to be a disaster. It very soon prompted retaliatory statutes in neighboring states to forbid state purchases from Minnesota producers. The first day of the next session, the chief author brought me another bill to coauthor, for a repeal of his success. Poor research! The lessons for me were in the failure to anticipate unforeseen consequences and to ask, "What may not work, and why?" or, "Has this been tried somewhere else and failed?"

No discussion of my failures would be complete without mentioning my Men's Right to Know bill, which I introduced in 1995. I drafted it to mock the Woman's Right to Know bill, backed by Minnesota Citizens Concerned for Life. That bill required "informed consent" for women seeking an abortion. It would force women to wait twenty-four hours between meeting with a doctor and receiving an abortion and to be told certain information, including available alternatives, which might discourage them from going through with the procedure.

My proposal would say that a man could not have a vasectomy without also waiting twenty-four hours. During that time, he had to inform his wife, her parents, and his parents about the impending procedure.[10]

The bill was a tease. I knew that an abortion and a vasectomy were not comparable, but I wanted to bring attention to the issue. Using the power the word "vasectomy" had with men seemed appropriate. Also I wanted the bill to be a surprise to the house Health and Human Services Committee, where it was sent after I introduced it. So I did not explain the bill to the committee majority or ask for their support at the first hearing. Nor did I enlist a senate author.

I testified at the house committee that "this is an important family issue." I told the panel I had been surprised by a son-in-law when he'd told me that he had just had a vasectomy. In my story, I'd said, "What? You just cut me off from any more grandchildren! You didn't tell me anything about it." "Too bad. It's my decision," he'd said, I told the committee.

After I finished my testimony, Republican representative Tony Onnen spoke. In 1985, he had been the committee chairman who had refused to give me a hearing on my living will bill unless I had the support of the MCCL lobbyist, Jackie Schwietz. Onnen now said, "I am going to vote for this because I think it is a good pro-family bill."

At this point, Republican representative Eileen Tompkins said, "Well, if Representative Onnen supports this, I will, too."

Then a Democratic majority member of the panel said, "I don't understand this bill, but if Representatives Onnen and Tompkins are for this, I will vote against it." So did another majority member.

In a completely surprising turn of events, my proposal on a Man's Right to Know lost in committee by just one vote.

However, my bill had caught the attention of people at the Canadian radio program *As It Happens*. They did a short piece on my bill. I started getting calls from all over the country and the proposal got a lot of attention. Dr. Spencer Payne, a Mayo Clinic surgeon who was a former law client and old friend, told me he had been in Scotland at a medical conference when a Scottish surgeon asked him where he lived. When Dr. Payne said, "Rochester, Minnesota," the Scot replied, "I think that is where a state legislator is from, the one I heard about on *As It Happens.* His bill required a twenty-four-hour wait for a vasectomy and that notice be given to the couple's parents."

"Yes," said Dr. Payne. "He was my lawyer."

This showed me the potential publicity I had lost by not lining up enough informed supporting votes at the committee hearing. This was a failure to use the rule I already knew was important: don't surprise those whose support you will need. Instead, I should have informed my colleagues and gotten them to commit their votes. If I had followed the right procedure, my proposal might have advanced to the Rules Committee and then to the full house. I might have gotten much broader exposure and been able to persuade more people that the Woman's Right to Know bill was an unreasonable restriction on women's choices. That had been my point all along.

As it was, MCCL eventually succeeded in getting the Woman's Right to Know bill enacted into law. This happened in 2003, after I retired. As I write this chapter, the law is still on the books.

{ Conclusion }

Finding common ground is essential to passing good legislation. Because a majority vote is required to enact a bill into public policy, a minority member can play a crucial role in crafting legislation and delivering votes. I achieved what I did in my career as a minority legislator because I built bridges to the majority. I generally stayed away from highly partisan tax and spending issues, though my caucus leadership knew I could be trusted to vote with them on such bills—so much so that I was made chair of the Ways and Means Committee for my last four years, when we had regained the majority. At the same time, I was free to work with members of the former majority party to effect important policy changes.

I was a witness to a changing political climate in the Minnesota legislature. During my tenure at the capitol, both caucuses collaborated on many nonpartisan bills, in a collegial atmosphere. Relationships were built on trust from both caucuses, and by work from both sides of the aisle, in a spirit of collaboration instead of confrontation.

In my first legislative session, I learned about working with the majority on good nonpartisan bills. I spent the first two hours of every day, five days a week, on the State Government Agency Appropriations Subcommittee chaired by

DFL representative Phyllis Kahn, who taught me a great deal about thorough legislative committee work done without partisanship. Such teaching must continue. Legislators of the future can learn from lawmakers of the past. It is essential that they reach across partisan boundaries. They must recognize colleagues as collaborators, not opponents. They should be reasonable, avoid most partisanship, and work together for the public good. If they do, the citizens will reward them.

Creating or changing laws should be hard work and include input from many sources. It should end with a bicameral and bipartisan win-win. Policymaking really does work, and work better, when it involves minority participation.

The best legislating involves people who are knowledgeable, share concerns, and are willing to be cooperative, whatever their party or caucus status.

The people of the state need to better understand the legislative process and respect the legislature for its work as the foundational arm of democratic government. People expect their legislators to be solons, wise people. They don't expect these officials to serve only one party or a single issue. They elect lawmakers to evaluate all issues and represent the general public to do the public good.

By the second decade of the twenty-first century, almost all of our legislative bodies, federal and state, are in virtual gridlock between excessively partisan majority and minority groups. Extremists on both sides are eager to attack those who would negotiate or compromise, threatening to withdraw support in the next campaign and to elect an even more partisan member. Genuine debate and multilateral deliberation are also too rare. When there is no trust, power is not shared, and legislating for the public good is secondary to partisan victories. Severe partisanship threatens the basic nature of democratic government.

But not so long ago, legislators found common ground between majority and minority in the pursuit and passage of legislation for the public good. This book shows how it's done. The people in our democracy need and deserve creative, courageous legislators who will consider this situation, and then take risks to do the right thing.

{ Afterword }

John Hughes

R eaders of the previous chapters now have a job to do.
Whether they are legislators, council members, aca-
demic experts, or voters, they need to take these lessons to
heart. Dave Bishop will consider this book a failure if it isn't
used to improve government.

But where to begin? After Bishop put forth so many strategies, tools, and ideas, which ones are priorities, and which is
the most important to seize as a first step?

The start is easy. People must make a personal decision
to embrace bipartisanship. That means working with both
sides of their board, council, or legislature—or supporting
candidates who do. Bishop makes clear that such an approach
won't happen by accident. It must be a choice, a part of a
strategy—a plan. It must be a purpose.

As I write this essay in my home in Washington, DC,
lawmakers at the Capitol three miles away have just com-
pleted another round of deadline brinksmanship. This time
the struggle was over the extension of federal funds for the
nation's highways—for three months. Yes, three months.
Even issues such as fixing roads, which historically have

been in the realm of the routine and mundane, have become exercises in partisanship and infighting.

This partisanship occurs not only among competing caucuses, but within them. As this happens, national approval ratings for the Congress drift ever lower.

Imagine if Congress members decided, instead of always seeking the political edge, to exercise the minimum amount of partisanship necessary. They could be partisan enough so that they manage to raise a sufficient amount of money and support to get elected. And they could be partisan enough to maintain respect within their caucus. But they would devote most of their energy to accomplishing policy through bipartisanship.

Bishop made a philosophical choice to make cross-party cooperation his norm of operation while occasionally demonstrating partisanship, rather than the other way around. And he proved it was a path to success.

"Minority members who want to pass bills and create good public policy can be very effective if they are willing to downplay their partisanship," Bishop writes.

Of course, once he made the choice to minimize partisanship, it wasn't always easy for Bishop to exist in what he terms "the bridge-building caucus." I wrote about Bishop for five years as a reporter at the state capitol for the *Rochester Post-Bulletin*. One of his regular sayings during that time was, "When you walk down the middle of the road, you get hit by the traffic going in both directions."

No caucus, either back then or today, is deeply fond of an independent-minded, bipartisan lawmaker. Caucus chiefs don't put centrists on the path to leadership. Being a middle-roader can be a lonely proposition. If it was an easy role, there would be many more bipartisan lawmakers in state houses throughout the country. Bodies such as Congress wouldn't be gridlocked to the extent they are. Solutions to tough issues wouldn't be postponed until the next generation.

Yet Bishop presents compelling evidence that, despite the challenges, bipartisanship brings superior results, particularly for people in minority caucuses. The evidence is his record of enacting scores of bills. And if that isn't persuasive enough, Bishop offers further validation—the very structure of government. The Constitution "creates genuine conflicts that must be resolved by negotiation and compromise," he writes.

Bishop as a legislator had tremendous trust in that structure. The legislative process for Bishop wasn't a maze to be circumvented or avoided. Rather, it was a framework that allowed a partisan to build, with thoughtful care, the elements necessary to achieve success for a policy idea.

In Bishop's view of legislating, every hearing was worth having. Each coauthor who could be signed up was mission critical. Every tweak of legislative language, no matter how small, was a difference maker. When it came to process, it all mattered, every step.

Through his examples of crafting the living will and sexual predator bills, Bishop shows the painstaking work he put forth. Whether it was lining up witnesses for hearings, connecting with outside groups for information, or persuading colleagues of the merits of the proposals, he realized each step needed careful execution. Rather than be dragged down by the lengthy and cumbersome process, he engaged in it with aplomb and enthusiasm.

In fact, Bishop's embrace of the process enabled his success. He mastered the mechanics of how legislation is enacted into law—and then spent years writing this book, so he could pass the knowledge along to others.

"I learned that the process itself is an important part of building the trust required to pass legislation," Bishop writes.

Shortcuts are tempting for policymakers. After all, who can resist a quick path to success? In Congress, one party often faults the other for circumventing the process with critical legislation. Howls of "we don't even know what's in this bill" can be heard on the floors of the House and Senate during crucial debates.

Bishop learned the hard way that taking a short cut was a risk he couldn't afford. Fresh from his victory with the living will bill, he was riding a bit high and mighty and decided he didn't need to widely vet his follow-up proposal on durable power of attorney. Soon, he felt the ire of senior groups, and his plan fell apart, though later he was able to piece it back together.

Failing to reach out to lawmakers, and taking support for granted, also doomed a proposed agreement, backed by Bishop, with the Mille Lacs Band of Ojibwe. It was a pitfall he saw repeated numerous times in his career. "I have seen the most powerful committee chairs propose significant bills and lose them because they didn't attempt to persuade anyone," he writes.

Aside from his few mistakes, persuasion was something

Bishop took seriously. He used to prowl around the capitol complex with vanilla-colored file folders that were bulging with paper scraps. He was always ready to whip out a newspaper article or other document, which he would foist toward a lawmaker or lobbyist he encountered in the hallway. (He also liked to carry cartoons and other written witticisms he could use for a laugh, or to disarm a critic.)

In his effort to persuade, getting information and support from outside groups was essential. He liked to go beyond what most lawmakers would consider their comfort area. He reached out to independent researchers, or journalists, or even opponents to get the information he needed.

"Unfortunately, many legislators rely only on their own caucus staff, receiving everything through a partisan filter," he writes.

Does all this process and persuasion that Bishop advocates extend the time it takes to reach success? Sure. Increasing the speed limit took seven years; passing the living will took five. Will the process cause frustration and require patience? Yes. Will it force compromise? Most definitely. But in the legislative results he describes, Bishop shows the effort is well worth it—even if pieces of legislation took years to complete, and they often did.

In this book, Bishop also shows that his embrace of bipartisanship and of the governing process opened avenues for him, and he believes it will do so for others. With this approach, the entirety of a legislature, council, or board, and all the regulations and procedures that govern it, become potential instruments in a vast toolbox. Like an artist, the policymaker is free to paint on an entire canvas, rather than being limited to a corner of it through a caucus or narrow process view.

Free of caucus restraints, Bishop roamed widely in the state capitol complex to satisfy his curiosity and interests. He played roles in issues he certainly didn't plan to pursue when he was first elected. He went beyond his personal agenda. He decided to get involved if he saw a need, and if he believed he could reach a successful end result.

"I spoke with bill authors, offered amendments, and was a source of support for legislation when I thought the basic purpose was good," he writes.

In the case of "Winning with the Lottery," Bishop describes how he wandered one day into the ornate retiring room behind the house chamber. He happened to be curious about a conversation two powerful Democratic colleagues were having. Not only did he inject himself into the conversation, but he also determined that he would engage on a new issue—the state lottery.

The result, of course, went beyond the initial success of the lottery bill. Through the collaboration, he built the beginning of a trusting friendship with one of the most accomplished Democrats in the Minnesota House, Willard Munger. Their partnership continued for years and encompassed numerous pieces of legislation.

Such "power sharing," as Bishop describes it, came about because of his willingness to help. He didn't limit himself based on party status or even his specific area of expertise. "Minority members make it easier for the majority to share power when they show support for and help the majority pass good nonpartisan bills," Bishop writes.

Where does one find these good bills that enable them to make a difference? People can't count on happenstance conversations in the house retiring room. Bishop says he got ideas from the governor's office, community organizations, and the general public. "It wasn't unusual for me to find ideas for legislation in the newspapers," he writes.

When he read about a horrific pipeline accident in his newspaper one morning, it could have ended there. He could have tucked the paper under his arm and gone to work to pursue one of his pet issues—the living will, perhaps, or a higher education need for his city of Rochester. Instead, he roamed. He picked up the phone, spoke with the governor, and said he wanted to play a role in an issue with which he had little or no experience: pipeline safety. He simply saw an opportunity to make a difference, and he seized it.

Roaming so broadly—taking on issues of less personal consequence—meant that his ego wasn't tied up in it. As a type of legislative freelancer, he was able to be a neutral arbiter of what was good and bad in a proposed piece of legislation or in a policy idea. In his role as a nonpartisan, he carried less risk than someone trying to protect his or her position in a caucus leadership structure. He was free of the cliques that can form within a caucus. Indeed, many Democrats no doubt viewed him as something of a novelty—a Republican willing to work with them. How unique, and how interesting, they might have thought.

Such alliances, even if they didn't result in long-term partnerships, often proved beneficial beyond the immediate bill they were built around. In the Northwest Airlines example, Bishop's generally helpful attitude in constructing nuances of the Northwest aid package later paid dividends in a sales-tax issue for his district. "I had built a bridge that was there when I needed it," he writes.

Being helpful to Democrats sometimes meant giving them credit. Sometimes, as a minority member, he had no choice in the matter. On other occasions, however, Bishop surrendered credit as part of a strategy.

"If I concluded that a proposal of mine needed a majority house author in order to pass in the senate, I would take it to a committee chair so he or she could get the credit," he writes.

He recounts the story of a bill he was working on with a majority colleague, Representative Randy Kelly. When the tables turned after an election, and Bishop suddenly found himself in the majority, Kelly was prepared to switch places and let Bishop take the lead on the bill. No, Bishop told him. "It's your idea and your work." The episode no doubt helped cement a partnership with Kelly that continued for many years.

Bishop writes that "the most important part of the bill is the final result, not the name of the individual who sponsored it." These are unusual words in an era when wealthy friends begin raising massive amounts of money for monumental libraries even before a president leaves office. So many leaders today seem focused on being remembered and on getting credit.

Yet maybe Bishop is on to something. Most people go through their lives without knowing who first thought to add sidewalks to their neighborhood, or who established a local park, or who came up with the idea for an education program that helped their children. Some unknown individuals did those great things, and people enjoy the benefit of them daily. Ultimately, that benefit seems more important than the name on a rusty plaque or a statue that collects bird droppings.

Now don't worry—if all this talk about helpfulness and selflessness seems a bit too, well, unpolitical, Bishop has some promising suggestions. Don't forget to be partisan! Yes, he writes, "partisan activities are legitimate political actions. Partisanship is part of the role of the minority."

There were plenty of examples of Bishop abandoning partisanship, such as when he backed a Democratic tax bill to achieve a local sales tax for his community. But he also looked for occasional ways to be partisan and bolster his Republican credentials, which go back to the days of Dwight Eisenhower.

"Legislators must work with their own caucus on critical issues such as taxes, budgets, and major financing bills. These issues usually define the philosophical and partisan divisions between the caucuses."

On the bonding bill conference committee, Bishop was a strong advocate for his Republican conference position. He also saw a way to simultaneously win something for his district and gain a personal priority.

Then there was Bishop's story of the deficiency bill and the massive Republican tax cut. In a twist of irony, after all his years of bipartisanship and working with Democrats, it was Bishop who stood up on the house floor and uttered these words: "I'm pleased to be the author of the now-largest income-tax cut in the history of the state."

Bishop as a legislator showed he was unusually bright and pragmatic, with an irascible charm and strong devotion to his home district. He was intensely energetic and wise about legislating. Yet, none of that matters. The point of all these examples, in these chapters, is that he discovered and employed tactics. Like the Mayo Clinic doctors who were his constituents, he chose specific tools and procedures to use at certain times to bring about success. It is these tools that he wants to hand to others. To the extent there is a focus on him or his personality, he would see that as diminishing the importance of the tools. He would tell everyone—don't do that.

So Bishop is suggesting that people use these approaches for a successful government: choose to be bipartisan; trust the process; be persuasive; look broadly when seeking information; find plentiful opportunities to be helpful; go beyond your immediate agenda; let others take credit; but don't forget to be partisan—at least once in a while.

Got it? Good. Now get busy. The democracy is counting on you all.

John Hughes, formerly a reporter for the *Rochester Post-Bulletin*, is editor for Bloomberg News's First Word and president of the National Press Club.

{ Acknowledgments }

In getting a final draft of this book ready to send to my publisher, I have had the benefit of editing counsel from many friends and relatives. Chief among these has been the dedicated attention of my daughter Marnie Bishop Elmer. John Hughes, an old friend and former reporter of my legislative work at the *Rochester Post-Bulletin*, put in many hours from his Washington, DC, home and helped me restructure the book and asked questions for clarifications. I also benefited from similar advice from my old and best legislative friend, Rick Krueger. My daughter Kathy; son, Tom; and wife, Bea, reviewed the manuscript and supplied corrections and suggestions. My granddaughter Angela Elmer helped me with editing and improvements. Lori Sturdevant and the late Jim Ragsdale of the *Minneapolis Star-Tribune* read my first manuscript and offered enthusiasm, as did Emily Shapiro, Tom Berg, Phyllis Kahn, and Amy Caucutt. Wes Skoglund provided text corrections. I am very grateful to these folks for their help.

{ Notes }

Notes to Preface

1. John Dunbar, "The 'Citizens United' Decision and Why It Matters," The Center for Public Integrity, October 18, 2012, http://www.publicintegrity.org/2012/10/18/11527/citizens-united-decision-and-why-it-matters.
2. Minnesota Legislature Reference Library, "Party Control of the Minnesota House of Representatives, 1951–Present," http://www.leg.state.mn.us/lrl/histleg/caucus.aspx?body=h; Dave Bishop, personal records of chief authorship, 1983–2002.

Notes to Chapter 1

1. Regent Candidate Advisory Council, "Report to the Minnesota Legislature" (1989); John Hughes, "Legislators Upset About Regent Process," Rochester Post-Bulletin, April 18, 1991.
2. Minnesota Historical Society, "Elmer Andersen Biography," http://collections.mnhs.org/governors/index.php/10004224.
3. Edie Grossfield, "Rochester Flood 35 Years Ago Brought Many Changes," Rochester Post-Bulletin, July 5, 2013.
4. Omnibus Tax Bill, Minnesota Session Laws (1983), Chapter 342, article 19, approved by Governor Perpich on June 14, 1983, House File No. 214–15.
5. Minnesota Department of Revenue, "Minnesota's Local Sales and Use Taxes: A Report to the 2004 Minnesota Legislature," February 2004, http://www.revenue.state.mn.us/research_stats/research_reports/2004/research_reports_content_local_sales_tax_study.pdf.

6. Steve Schultze and Ron Freeberg, "Legislators Close Out Session," *Rochester Post-Bulletin*, n.d.
7. Steve Schultze, "Conferees Agree to Include City 'Piggyback' Tax," *Rochester Post-Bulletin*, n.d.; Minnesota Department of Revenue, "Minnesota Tax Handbook: A Profile of State and Local Taxes in Minnesota" (2010), http://www.revenue.state .mn.us/research_stats/research_ reports/2010/2010_handbook.pdf.

Notes to Chapter 2

1. Gary Dawson, "House Passes Bill To Have Lottery Vote," *St. Paul Pioneer Press*, April 7, 1988; Janice Gregorson, "Bishop Attacks IR Chairman for His Anti-Lottery Position," *Rochester Post-Bulletin*, May 21, 1988.
2. Dawson, "House Passes Bill to Have Lottery Vote."
3. Grant Moos, "Approved Bill Wasn't Like One Bishop Crafted," *Rochester Post-Bulletin*, April 21, 1988.
4. John Hughes, "Lawmakers Friendlier Toward New Mille Lacs Deal," *Rochester Post-Bulletin*, April 23, 1993.
5. Robert Whereatt, "House Rejects Mille Lacs Plan; Chippewa to Take Case to Court," *Minneapolis Star-Tribune*, May 4, 1993.

Notes to Chapter 3

1. House File No. 1866 (1990).
2. Center for Policy Alternatives, Jeffery Tryens and Bill Rice, eds., "Best Bets: 1990 Model State Environmental Actions," *Policy Alternatives on Environment: A State Report* 7.3 (September 1990).
3. Unidentified, undated newspaper clipping in author's files.
4. Minnesota Department of Human Services, "Report to the Commissioner: Commitment Act Task Force" (1988); Minnesota Psychiatric Society, "Problems with the Current Psychopathic Personality Statute" (1992); Dave Bishop, "Understanding the Proposed Sexual Predator Law," *Rochester Post-Bulletin*, August 30, 1994.
5. "Fighting Sex Crimes," *Session Weekly* 12.9 (March 3, 1995).

6. Minnesota Department of Human Services, "Report to the Commissioner: Commitment Act Task Force," 1988.
7. Minnesota Department of Human Services, "Report to the Commissioner."
8. Natalie Haas Steffen, letter to author, September 13, 1991; Minnesota Psychiatric Society, "Problems with the Current Statute."
9. Minnesota Supreme Court regarding Phillip Blodgett, January 14, 1994.
10. Donna Halvorsen, "Sex Predators' Status Sparks Insecurity," *Minneapolis Star-Tribune*, July 9, 1994.
11. Dave Bishop, "Sexual Predator Law," speech, Rochester, MN, 1994.
12. Bishop, "Sexual Predator Law."
13. "Task Force of Sexual Predators: Final Report to the Minnesota Legislature," January 4, 1995.
14. Arne Carlson, "State of Minnesota Proclamation," August 29, 1994.
15. Donna Halvorsen and Robert Whereatt, "Sexual Predator Bill OK'd, Signed," *Minneapolis Star-Tribune*, September 1, 1994.

Note to Chapter 4

1. Bill Marx, phone conversation with author, Rochester, MN, April 22, 2014.

Notes to Chapter 5

1. Metropolitan Airports Commission, "Airports Commission, Northwest Airlines Negotiators Reach Agreement on Terms of Loan to Northwest," November 11, 1991; Minnesota Commissioner of Finance, "NWA Maintenance and Repair Facilities: Report to the Governor and Legislative Update," March 17, 1992.
2. John Hughes, "Package Raises Questions: Frustration Surrounds Northwest Deal," *Rochester Post-Bulletin*, November 14, 1991.
3. William C. Boyne, "Bishop Asks Long-Range Look at State's

Finances," *Rochester Post-Bulletin*, March 3, 1987; Minnesota Session Laws (1986), Chapter 3.
4. Bruce Orwall, "Vote on NWA Loan to be 'Very Close,'" *St. Paul Pioneer Press*, December 15, 1991.
5. David Phelps and Robert Whereatt, "Northwest Deal Approved: Legislative Panel OKs $320 Million MAC Loan: NWA, Taxpayers Uniquely Linked," *Minneapolis Star-Tribune*, December 17, 1991.

Notes to Chapter 6

1. National Transportation Safety Board, "Williams Pipeline Company: Liquid Pipeline Rupture and Fire: Moundsview, MN: July 8, 1986," NTSB/PAR-87/02, July 20, 1987.
2. Pipeline Safety Act, HF0091, SF 0090 (June 2, 1987); Office of Pipeline Safety, Minnesota Department of Public Safety, "Fact Sheet," 2013.
3. Ron Drevlow, "Bill Would Tighten Law on Drug Deaths," *Rochester Post-Bulletin*, April 1, 1987; "Prohibition of Sexual Solicitation of Children," Minnesota Session Laws (1986), Chapter 445, House File No. 1835.
4. Donna Dunn, letter to author, October 18, 1983.
5. John Hughes, "A Safe Place for Asian Women," *Rochester Post-Bulletin*, December 16, 1993.
6. Olmsted County Board of Commissioners, meeting notes, February 27, 1983.
7. Thomas Keliher, transcript of retirement speech, May 2002.
8. Chris Herlinger, "Pro-Choice Group Going to 'Play Hardball' with MCCL," *Rochester Post-Bulletin*, December 4, 1987.
9. Dave Bishop, memo, January 9, 1989.
10. Howard Orenstein, Dave Bishop, Leigh D. Mathison, "Minnesota's Living Will," *The Bench & Bar of Minnesota* (August 1989).

Notes to Chapter 7

1. Grant Moos, "Bishop Amendment Limits Bonding Bills," *Rochester Post-Bulletin*, April 7, 1988.

2. "Legislative Commission on Fiscal Policy, Government Operations," Minnesota Session Laws (1988), House File No. 0547.
3. Elmer L. Andersen, "Saving the Historical Society," *Princeton Union-Eagle*, March 29, 1984.
4. Beth Dunlop, "Judicious Decision: Jury Picks Courthouse Design," *Miami Herald*, March 31, 1985.
5. Conference Committee Report on House File No. 919, May 18, 1987.

Notes to Chapter 8

1. Surface Transportation and Uniform Relocation Assistance Act of 1987, Pub. L. 100–17, 101 Stat. 132, April 2, 1987; National Highway System Designation Act of 1995, Pub. L. 104–59, 109 Stat. 568, November 28, 1995.
2. US Department of Transportation, "Effects of Raising and Lowering Speed Limits," October 1992.
3. Minnesota Department of Highways, "Construction Plan," March 1953.
4. US Department of Transportation, "Effects of Raising and Lowering Speed Limits."
5. Minnesota Management and Budget, "Spending History, 1960 to Present, May 2014: Historical Expenditures: General Fund and All Funds," June 27, 2014.
6. Bill McAuliffe, "GOP Split Sinks Spending Bill," *Minneapolis Star-Tribune*, April 7, 1999; Jim Ragsdale, "Routine Bill Fails Over Split in Party," *St. Paul Pioneer Press*, April 7, 1999.
7. Patricia Lobex Baden and Bill McAuliffe, "House Unites in Tax Surprise," *Minneapolis Star-Tribune*, April 14, 1999.
8. Minnesota House of Representatives Public Information Office, "New Laws 1999 Session Summary."
9. Ron Drevlow, "Polite but Firm Bikers Cheer Defeat of Another Helmet Bill," *Rochester Post-Bulletin*, March 5, 1987.
10. Robert Whereatt, "Proposal Would Require 1-Day Wait to get Vasectomy," *Minneapolis Star-Tribune*, January 27, 1995.

{ Index }

Page numbers in *italics* indicate photographs.

administrative-law judges, 54
Allen, Ernie, 47–48
alliances. *See* bridge-building
Almanac, 70
Amdahl, Doug, 103, 105
Andersen, Elmer, 10
Anderson, Irv, 30, 31
Anderson, Wendell, 115
Appropriations Committee, 59, 81, 102, 104, 106
Armey, Dick, 53
Arthur, Lindsay, 41

Backus, Ken, 53
Battaglia, David, 29–30, 32, 104–6
battered women's shelters, 80–82
Beard, Pat, 126
Beecher, Lee, 39, 41
Belau, Jane, 69–70
Bergstrom, Greg, 55–56
Betzold, Don, 53, 54–55
bicameral legislatures, xv, 17
bills: coauthors of, 84–85; germaneness principal, 113, 119; ideas for, 79–83,

141; offering amendments for vs. voting against, 4–6; strategies for passing, 84–89; timing of, 112–13; vehicles for, 85–86; voting on, 112; wording of, 113–14. *See also specific bills*
Bishop, Bea Habberstad, ix
Bishop, Dave, *xiv, 82*; background of, ix; bipartisan lawmaking focus, viii–ix, xii, xvii–xix; at GOP convention (1980), x–xi; law practice, 3–4, 40; post–9/11 state budget plan, vii–viii
Blodgett, Phillip, 42
Bloomer, Barbara, 26, 27
bonding bills, 60, 61–67
Brataas, Nancy, 72–73, 76
bridge-building, 17–32, 140; "dancing" with majority party, 99–102; legislator's homework for, 109–10; Minnesota State Lottery case, 20–26; strategies for, 17–20; trust and, 26–32
Bush, George H. W., xi

Capitol Area Architecture and
   Planning Board, 106
capitol building, 103–4
Carlson, Arne, 30, 45, 46, 56,
   62, 73, 82, 117–18
Carlson, Doug, 14
Carruthers, Phil, 43
Catholic Health Association, 95
Catholic organizations, 94–95
Caucutt, Amy, 86
Center for Policy Alternatives,
   39
child sexual abuse bill, 80
Citizens United decision, xvi
Clark, Karen, 81
coalitions. *See* bridge-building
Commitment Act, Minnesota,
   40
communication, 88
community-notification bill,
   46–56
compromise, 17–18
conference committees, 57–67
Conner, John, 117
constituent protection, 10–15
constituent services, 109
controlled substances bill, 80
Corrections, Minnesota Department of, 42, 44, 48, 53,
   55
counterlegislation, 114–15
county attorneys, 43, 53–56

"dancing," by legislatures,
   99–102
deficiency bill (1999), 119–25
democracy, xv, 8, 33

Dempsey, Jerry, 64
Department of Corrections, 42,
   44, 48, 53, 55
Department of Human Ser-
   vices, 40, 42, 44
Department of Natural Re-
   sources (DNR), 29, 64
Department of Transportation,
   116, 118–19
diversionary tactics, 114–15
domestic abuse, 80–82
Dorn, John, 65
Duluth, bonding bills benefit-
   ing, 60
Dunn, Donna, 81
durable power of attorney,
   26–29, 126

Eagle Creek, 64–65
Environmental and Natural
   Resources Trust Fund, 22,
   24, 25
Erdahl, Arlen, 10
Erickson, Jim, 76

failures, 125–29
Fearing, Jerry, 107
fishing rights, Mille Lacs Band
   of Ojibwe, 29–32
flood control project, Rochester
   (1983), 10–15
Foley, Leo, 117
Frerichs, Don, 14, 63
Fridley, Russ, 103, 105, 106

germaneness, principal of, 113,
   119

Gilbert, Cass, 103, 104
Glumac, Ann, 38
Greater Minnesota Corpora-
    tion, 22–23, 25
Greenfield, Lee, 39, 40, 41, 53
Greenfield, Marcia, 52
Groundwater Protection Act,
    Minnesota, 37–39
Guelker, Bill, 55
Gutknecht, Gil, 11, 13–14, 73,
    76

Habiger, James, 95
Halberg, Chuck, 36–37
health care: durable power of
    attorney, 26–29; living wills,
    89–97
Health Committee, 90–91
Henderson, Julie, 51
higher education, 63–67
homework, legislator's, 109–10
Hughes, Jerry, 74, 100
Hughes, John, 43
Human Services, Minnesota
    Department of, 40, 42, 44
Humphrey, Skip, 41
hunting rights, Mille Lacs Band
    of Ojibwe, 29–32

ideas, for legislation, 79–97,
    141; living will case, 89–97;
    moving into law, 84–89;
    sources of, 79–83

Jacob Wetterling Foundation,
    51
Jaros, Mike, 27, 28

Jennings, David, 36, 89–90, 106
Jepsen, Cindy, 30–31
Jerichs, Ron, 76
Johnson, Doug, 73, 74, 75,
    76–77
journalists, building relation-
    ships with, 69–77
Judicial Center, 102–7
judicial office vacancies, 35–37
Judiciary Committee, 37, 49,
    56, 91–92, 94, 96
Judiciary Finance Committee,
    34, 49
Junge, Ember Reichgott, 27–28,
    75, 76, 93, 94

Kahn, Phyllis, 59, 103, 132
Kalis, Henry, 38
Keliher, Tom, 74, 87
Kelly, Randy, 35–37, 49–50,
    52–53, 55, 66, 91, 94, 142
Kinkel, Tony, 65–66
Kiscaden, Sheila, 65
Krueger, Rick, 24, 60–61

Lake Mille Lacs, 29
Lake Superior Railroad
    Museum, 105
Langseth, Keith, 117
Legislative-Citizen Commis-
    sion on Minnesota Re-
    sources, 100
Legislative Commission on
    Planning and Fiscal Policy
    (LCPFP), 73–76, 101
legislators: bridge-building
    by, 17–32; power sharing

by, 33–56, 140; priorities
of, xviii–xix; toolbox for,
109–15, 139
Leier, Marsie, x
Lieb, Roxanne, 47
Lincoln, Abraham, xv
Linehan, Dennis, 44, 46
living will bill, 89–97
lobbying, 110–11
Long, Dee, 75, 76
Lottery, Minnesota State,
20–26
Ludeman, Cal, 36

majority control, 33
Marx, Bill, 120
Men's Right to Know bill
(1995), 127–29
Merriam, Gene, 65, 66
Metropolitan Airports Com-
mission, 73
Michaels, Jean, 37
Mille Lacs Band of Ojibwe,
29–32
Miller, Judy, 81, 82
Minneapolis Police Depart-
ment, 48
Minneapolis Star Tribune, viii
Minneapolis Tribune, x
Minnesota Association of
Townships, 115
Minnesota Catholic Confer-
ence, 94–95
Minnesota Citizens Concerned
for Life (MCCL), 28, 90–93,
95–96, 120, 127, 128, 129

Minnesota Commitment Act,
40
Minnesota County Attorneys
Association, 43
Minnesota Groundwater Protection Act, 37–39
Minnesota Historical Society
move, 102–7
Minnesota History Center, 107
Minnesota Judicial Center,
102–7
Minnesota producers, bill
requiring state and local governments to purchase from,
126–27
Minnesota Psychiatric Association, 39–40
Minnesota Psychiatric Society,
42
Minnesota Security Hospital,
40, 42, 44
Minnesota State Capitol,
103–4
Minnesota State Lottery,
20–26, 140
Minnesota State Patrol, 116,
117, 118
Minnesota Supreme Court, 43,
44
Minnesota Zoo, 120, 121, 122,
125
minority parties: bridge-
building with majority,
17–20; "dancing" with
majority party, 99–102;
offering amendments to bills

vs. voting against, 4–6, 8–9; power sharing with majority, 33–39; role of, 8–9, 131
Moe, Roger, 7
motorcycle helmet bill, 125–26
Mounds View, underground pipeline accident (1986), 79–80
Munger, Willard, 20–22, 24–26, 38, 60, 140
Murphy, Mary, 34

NAACP, lawsuits against schools, 120, 121, 122
National Center for Missing and Exploited Children, 48
National Highway Traffic Safety Administration, 117, 118
National Right to Life Committee, 92
Natural Resources, Minnesota Department of, 29, 64
Neel, Bryan, 7
negotiation, 9, 59–60
Neuville, Tom, 54–55
news media, 69–77. See also specific newspapers
Northwest Airlines, 73–77
Novak, Steve, 80

Oberstar, James, 76, 77
omnibus bills, 86
O'Neill, Joe, 95
Onnen, Tony, 90, 128
Orenstein, Howard, 28

Orwall, Bruce, 74
Ostrom, John, 65

Parker, Leonard, 103, 106
partisanship, problem of, xv–xvii, 3–10
Pawlenty, Tim, vii–viii, 31, 124
Payne, Spencer, 128–29
Pelowski, Gene, 65
Penny, Tim, 10, 14
Perpich, Rudy, 14, 22, 25, 37, 79, 96, 105–6, 126–27
persistence, 112
personal touches, lawmaker's use of, 111–12
persuasion, 34, 109, 138–39
pipelines, underground, 79–80
Popovich, Peter, 105, 106
power sharing, 33–56, 140; community-notification law, 46–56; Groundwater Protection Act example, 37–39; judicial office vacancy bill example, 35–37; sexual-predator bill, 39–46; strategies for, 33–35
press releases, 72
Price, Len, 38
pro-life organizations, 28, 90–93, 95–96, 120, 127, 128, 129
Psychiatric Association, Minnesota, 39–40
Psychiatric Society, Minnesota, 42
Pugh, Tom, 122–24
Pung, Orville, 41

Quie, Al, x
Quist, Allen, 93

Reagan, Ronald, x–xi, 10
Redalen, Elton, 38
Regulated Industries and Energy Committee, 80
relationships, importance of, 19–20
reporters, building relationships with, 69–77
Republican Convention (Detroit, 1980), x–xi
Reynen, Penny, 66
Rickmyer, Peter, 44, 46
Rochester, MN: flood control project, 10–15; sales tax renewal (1990), 72–77
Rochester Post-Bulletin, 43, 69
Rochester University Center, 63–67
Rolvaag, Karl, 10
Rules Committee, 21–22, 24–25

Schmitz, Ray, 53–54, 56, 80
Schwietz, Jackie, 28, 90–91, 96, 128
Seck, Jerry, 66
senior citizens, 27, 28, 91, 93, 96–97
sexual-predator bills, 39–56
Shapiro, Emily, 42–43, 54, 55
Sheran, Robert, 10
Shilling, Bob, 51–52

Sieben, Harry, 12–13, 14, 36
Simoneau, Wayne, 21, 59, 101
Skoglund, Wes, 43, 45–46, 48, 52, 55–56
social events, 19–20
Solberg, Loren, 67
Solon, Sam, 60
Spear, Allan, 43, 44, 49, 52, 54–55
speed limit change, 115–19
State Office Building, 104
State Patrol, 116, 117, 118
Steffen, Natalie, 42
St. Paul Dispatch, 107
St. Paul Pioneer Press, 74, 75
Stuart, John, 54–55
Supreme Court, Minnesota, 43, 44
Supreme Court, US, xvi, 32
surrogate parenting bill, 126
Sviggum, Steve, 36, 63–64, 119–20, 123–24
Swan, Art, 3

taxation: Rochester flood control project levy, 11–15; Rochester sales tax (1990), 72–77; tax cut bill (1999), 123–24, 125
Tax Committee, 73, 77
timing, 112–13
Tompkins, Eileen, 128
townships, 115
Transportation, Minnesota Department of, 116, 118–19

Truman, Harry, 102
trust, importance in
  bridge-building, 26–32

underground pipelines, 79–80
United States Supreme Court:
  Citizens United decision,
  xvi; Mille Lacs Band of
  Ojibwe case, 32
University of Minnesota re-
  gents, 6–7

Valan, Merlyn, 57–58
Vanasek, Bob, 7–8
Vellenga, Kathleen, 39, 40, 41
Ventura, Jesse, 120, 123, 125
Voss, Gordy, 100
voting, 112

Wafler, Jim, 30
walleye fishing, Lake Mille
  Lacs, 29–32
Ways and Means Committee,
  119–20, 121, 131
Welker, Ray, 36
Wetterling, Patty, 48, 51
Wolf, Ken, 63–64, 67
Women's Right to Know bill,
  127–29
Women's Shelter, Inc., 81
Workman, Tom, 31
Wynia, Ann, 24

Yetka, Lawrence, 105, 106

Zoo, Minnesota, 120, 121, 122,
  125

{ Picture Credits }

pages xiv, 82: author's collection
page 12: History Center of Olmsted County
page 23: Minnesota Historical Society
page 107: courtesy Jerry Fielding

Finding Common Ground has been typeset in
Trump Mediaeval, an Old Face font developed by
Georg Trump between 1954 and 1962.

Book design and composition by Wendy Holdman.